Economy of Grace

ECONOMY of GRACE

KATHRYN TANNER

FORTRESS PRESS
MINNEAPOLIS

Library of Congress Cataloging-in-Publication Data

Tanner, Kathryn
    Economy of grace / Kathryn Tanner.
        p. cm.
    Includes bibliographical references and index.
    ISBN 0-8006-3774-7 (pbk : alk. paper)
    1. Economics—Religious aspects—Christianity 2. Capitalism—Religious aspects—Christianity. Title.
    BR115.E3T28 2005
    261.8'5—dc22
                                              2005010156

Everyone who thirsts, come to the waters;
and you that have no money, come, buy and eat!
Come, buy wine and milk without money and without price.
—Isaiah 55:1

Jesus . . . cried out, "Let anyone who is thirsty come to me,
and . . . drink."
—John 7:37-38

For as the rain and the snow come down from heaven,
and do not return there until they have watered the earth,
making it bring forth and sprout,
giving seed to the sower and bread to the eater,
so shall my word be that goes out from my mouth;
it shall not return to me empty,
but it shall accomplish that which I purpose,
and succeed in the thing for which I sent it.
—Isaiah 55:10-11

CONTENTS

PREFACE

The economy dominates our world today as never before, for better or worse. Economic goods bring every other sort with them. If you have money, you can have a good education, good health care, the respect of one's peers, a political post, and so on. And therefore every other sort of good is often simply geared to gaining the goods of wealth and economic security. What is an excellent education worth, for example, if it doesn't mean a well-paying job upon graduation? In short, all goods in our world tend to turn on the hinge of money—as either what brings money or what money buys.

Because all goods revolve in these ways around economic goods, economic ruin threatens to bring the whole of life down with it—not just for individuals but whole societies. Political and social ends are therefore commonly subordinated to, or disciplined by, economic ones. A leftist government or social policies to strengthen the welfare state risk capital flight to more business-friendly climes. And what could be more disastrous? No capital investment means no jobs, no money, no future.

This dominance, this discipline exerted by the economy, is often harsh. Our world seems at the mercy of fickle and unsparing economic winds. Cycles of boom and bust roil even the most advanced economies of East Asia and the United States. The impoverished and debtor nations of Africa and Latin America appear caught in irremediable spirals of devastating economic decline.

Since the economy is so central to our lives and the stakes are so high, Christians might hope that their religion would have a great deal to say about it. Wouldn't it indeed be wonderful if Christianity had its own vision of economic life, one opposed to the inhumanities of the present system and offering direction in trying times, a practical path to a better world? This book makes the case that Christianity does have an economic vision for the whole of life. That vision provides a radical alternative to the present system, and it suggests a practical program for change.

As a constructive theologian I want to promote a way of telling the Christian story and its vision of economy that will bring out its great contrast with the economic principles that rule the world of our experience. There is no point in looking to theology for insight on economic questions if theology merely ratifies the economic principles that the wider society takes for granted anyway. The greater the contrast, the greater the potential significance of turning to theology for economic suggestions—especially so in times like today, when the economic principles that our world abides by seem both to exhaust our imaginations and to be running amok.

My thesis rests on a conversation between theology and economics using a method of *comparative* or *general economy*. It is common in other literature on theology and economics to make economics a religious matter: theology and economics can converse because economics has its own gods, its own ultimate concerns of a broadly religious character, which theology is therefore entitled to critique. But my strategy is the reverse. Both conversation partners—theology and economics—are considered under the rubric of "economy" in a very broad sense, and that is what allows them to be considered together so directly. On the one side, there is theological economy, made up of fundamental principles for the production and circulation of goods as those are exhibited in the Christian story of God and the world; on the other side, there is economy in the more usual, narrow sense, the principles governing, for example, financial transactions, industrial production, competitive pricing, and so on. Theology and economics enter the same universe of discourse—discourse on economy—and can be directly compared on that basis.

The first chapter elicits the way in which the whole Christian story is a vision of economy, a vision of a kind of system for the production and circulation of goods, beginning with God and extending to the world, from creation through redemption. In this way of looking at the Christian story, Christianity is every bit as much about economic issues as an account of the way prices are determined by marginal utilities. The Christian story, after all, is a story about God as the highest good, a God constituted by exchange among the persons of the Trinity, a God who aims, in creating and saving the world, to distribute to it the good of God's own life to the greatest degree possible. Fundamentally at stake in this story are principles for the production and circulation of the good and what they are to mean for human life in God's service.

The method I offer in this first chapter for discussing theology and economics together is designed to allow for the maximum possible contrast between the economic principles the world follows and those involved in the Christian story of creation, fall, and redemption. My attempt to avoid a reductionistic method is motivated by such a concern. The Christian story may be a story of economy, but that does not mean it has to mirror any of the economies, in a narrower sense, with which we are familiar—barter, commodity exchange, debtor/creditor relations, and so forth. Historically, one might not find very often much of a contrast between the economic practices of the wider world and the principles of economy embedded in the way the Christian story is told (theological economy in my sense). But the method for bringing the two into conversation should not prejudge this matter or the degree to which a theological economy can fall out of sync with the economic principles of the wider society.

The second chapter fulfills the promise of this nonreductive, comparative method. It fills out in greater detail the principles of a theological economy as a radical alternative to the present system, with reference to other possible alternative principles of economy derived from historical and anthropological study. A theological economy is set into the mix of other efforts, which use the pre-history of capitalism in the West or the economic practices of nonindustrialized societies, to imagine alternatives to a capitalist economy now without rivals from either communist or socialist states.

The apparently utopian character of a theological economy might make one question its viability. How, one might ask, could an economy this different from anything we know ever be instituted? The third chapter counters these suspicions by showing theological economy's practical force, the way it allows one to get a handle on the present system of global capitalism, uncovering its weak points and offering realistic suggestions for a new way forward.

Acknowledgments

These chapters enjoyed a complicated history prior to their very thorough revision for inclusion here. And I would like to take this opportunity to thank all the institutions who sponsored them and all the many people, too many indeed to list, who listened and responded to their oral delivery or who commented on them in written form. A version of chapter 2 was the first to be written, during the years 1996–2000, as my contribution to William Schweiker's Lilly-funded interdisciplinary workshop on "Property, Possession, and the Theology of Culture." It appeared as "Economies of Grace" in *Having: Property and Possession in Religious and Social Life*, edited by William Schweiker and Charles Mathewes (Grand Rapids: Eerdmans, 2002). This essay was also discussed at the Erasmus Institute Workshop at the University of Notre Dame in 1999. The essay that makes up chapter 1 was originally written for delivery as the Lentz Lecture at Harvard Divinity School in 2002 and subsequently published in the *Harvard Divinity Bulletin* (spring 2002). A shorter version formed the material for a lunchtime talk around the same time at Yale Divinity School. The three essays came together for the first time as the Thomas White Currie Lectures at Austin Presbyterian Theological Seminary in 2003 and later that year were compressed into two for the Cole Lectures at Vanderbilt Divinity School. Much the same two lectures were given again at Garrett-Evangelical Theological Seminary in 2004, one at the invitation of the Stead Center for Ethics and Values and the other for a conference on faith, hope, and love to honor Nancy Bedford.

A version of chapter 3 was included for discussion at the "American Empire?" Conference at Drew University Theological School in 2003 and delivered as a public lecture at the University of Utrecht in 2004.

I would also like to thank the students at the University of Chicago who participated in a public theology workshop, during which the text of the Lentz lecture was discussed, and especially those who took part in a course on "Grace and Money," in which all three lectures were read. The later theological portions of chapter 2 follow closely material in chapter 3 of my *Jesus, Humanity, and the Trinity: A Brief Systematic Theology* (Minneapolis: Fortress Press, 2001), but far less closely than they did in the earlier version of the essay that appeared in *Having*.

This book is dedicated to the memory of my father, James John Tanner, who died in 1994. From his earnings as an accountant, he helped support me throughout the many years of my schooling, until I started to teach full-time in the religious studies department of Yale University in 1985. He always suspected that I did not fully appreciate the value of a dollar, and now there is proof.

1

AN ECONOMY OF GRACE?

Does Christianity really have very much to say directly about economic matters? That should be our first question in this chapter, since securing a positive answer to it is a prerequisite for the whole project. The easy answer is no, not much, not in any very direct manner. The primary burden of my method is to refute this presumption and allow one to see the way that every theological category and topic is of direct economic import, how every Christian idea about God and the world is directly and from the first an economic doctrine.

In my book *Theories of Culture* I suggest that theological ideas are always internally constituted by a contestatory relationship with the beliefs and practices of the wider world in which Christians live.[1] Christian beliefs and practices are the ideas and practices of that wider world taken up and transformed, made odd; they are therefore fashioned in and through an implicit critical commentary on the socio-cultural presumptions and practices of the wider society. Because of the way the ordinary assumptions of human life are altered in Christian use, when Christians say (for example) that God is love, they are saying something not just about God but about love, its true character, what's missing from love as we know it. And when Christians make meal fellowship a primary sacramental means of communing with Christ, something is being said not only about the character of Christ's incorporation of human beings but about the inadequacies of ordinary table fellowship—its exclusions, its use in enforcing arbitrary social divisions. There is no reason to think the same sort of process of

Christian belief and practice formation does not extend to economic matters.

What Has Christianity to Do with Economics?

One of the most salient features of the wider world, especially in our day, is its economic character. The wider world has its principles for the production of goods or, more generally, for the creation of value, and its principles for the distribution and exchange, the circulation, of such goods. Every theological category and claim, no matter how basic and theologically primary—say, the very idea of who and what God is—might very well then be framed, from the very beginning, in response to these economic principles of the wider world; any theological category might take up those economic principles, in the effort to make sense of God, and, by giving them an odd spin, offer, at least implicitly, a critical commentary on them.

But my own previous work notwithstanding, one might suppose with good reason that a very small number of rather secondary Christian claims have anything to do directly with economic issues. For example, historically the Christian church criticized usury—interest-bearing loans—but this criticism tended to fall away after the Reformation. Christians in the Radical Reformation minority made an appeal to the so-called primitive communism of the early church, which suggested an economic ideal of commonly held property. There are occasional attacks on money in Christian history—for example, among ascetics who withdrew to the desert in the first few centuries c.e. and among members of the early Franciscan movement, who refused, despite their living in the world, to engage in monetary transactions or to own real property. The Jubilee traditions in the Hebrew Bible and their extension into the New Testament promote the idea of an at least periodic forgiveness of the debt on loans. And there is of course a long-standing tradition of Christian concern about the corrupting influence of wealth and concern for the poor and the economically depressed, a concern that figures centrally in contemporary liberation theologies.

But this attention to economic issues often seems a mere second tier of theological concern, an optional addition or supplement to those strictly God-oriented questions that form theology's central domain. Direct attention to economic questions also emerges only piecemeal in Christian history, as occasions warrant, without any clear systematic connection among the various Christian pronouncements and warnings. It is therefore hard to make out in this scattered attention to economic questions any fundamental proposal for a whole economic way of life. And what the main theological claims of Christianity have to do with these economic judgments often remains rather opaque. For example, making money from money by exacting interest may be condemned in favor of wealth generated by hard work, but what does the latter demand for labor have to do with any fundamentally Christian claim about God or Jesus or life under God?

One common strategy for extending the economic relevance of Christianity beyond this history of rather limited direct comment and for enhancing Christianity's systematic economic import is to highlight fundamental Christian values. The focus becomes such Christian mainstays as love for neighbor, respect for the dignity of the human person, and repudiation of envy and greed in relations with others. Any one of those values might affect the whole of life, anchoring and centering it, and therefore help give a Christian economic perspective a systematic cast.

This strategy can easily suggest, however, that Christianity is primarily concerned with personal morals and not in any direct way with the structures and organization of economic life. The way societies are arranged is not Christianity's business; only the inward dispositions and attitudes of the individuals who populate them. The result is an overly individualistic approach to complicated structural issues. The moral transformation of the individuals engaged in economic transactions tends to become, for example, the answer to economic problems: if only our greedy CEOs were saints! The institutional and communal formation of human persons is downplayed in the process: CEOs inflate their profits because they are bad people; overlooked are the pressures built into a system that forces companies raising capital on the stock market to compete for money with the enormously lucrative short-term profits to be made in financial markets—for example, in currency speculation. Virtuous economic actors would no doubt be a good thing and have a profound effect, if not on the fundamental organizing principles of economic life, then on the ends to which it is dedicated and on the limits that must not be crossed in the pursuit of profit. It is a long way, however, from employees and employers who love one another to an entire economy of love. If one follows the norm of neighbor love, how might the goods that serve material needs be produced and distributed differently? How might the fundamental structures of economic life be reorganized in accordance with neighbor love? A focus on Christian virtue does not seem directly to suggest very much about any of that.

A similar complaint about indirection can be lodged against another common strategy for bringing out Christianity's enormous import for economic life. Every Christian claim is relevant to economic matters—not just the ones that directly comment on economic issues—since every Christian claim has a potential influence on the course of economic action that people will find reasonable and be motivated to pursue.[2] The stress here is on the complex way that Christian beliefs and commitments function in people's lives. For example, the belief that God loves every single person or the belief in Christ's second coming can have economic import, despite the fact that neither says anything on its face about wealth or poverty. These beliefs might provide, respectively, a sense of self-worth in the meantime and hope for a final reversal of fortune at the end-time, and in that way they might help those in dire economic straits bear up under capitalist discipline. Again the influence on economic life is rather indirect—by implication more than by any immediate Christian message of an economic sort—and passes (for all the possible attention to class consciousness or shared economic circumstance) through the individual's affects and attitudes. Even more than the previous strategy I mentioned, this one can give the impression—through the idea of unintended consequences—that Christian concerns are not fundamentally economic at all. Christianity might completely ignore the economic and still be of enormous economic importance. This is the famous line of argument in Max Weber's *The Protestant Ethic and the Spirit of Capitalism*.[3] Protestants are completely uninterested in making money to increase their material comfort, and they avoid conspicuous consumption for religious reasons. But the result is money saved and a willingness to invest it in productive enterprises; Protestants become rich, then, despite themselves, almost to the chagrin of their primary religious motives. Similarly, Protestantism disciplines the whole of life according to rigorous and uncompromising standards; everyone is expected to be a saint, and there are no accommodations made for backsliders (for example, penance won't get you off the hook). The result is people who are the perfect subjects for capitalist discipline; practice in tallying up one's wicked thoughts and actions against one's holy ones can be transferred to the debits and credits of the accountant's ledger. Finally, the emphasis on the way religious beliefs function, on their effects, distracts attention from the way the content of those beliefs might themselves be outlining a possible structure for economic affairs.

In contrast to these two strategies, which bring together Christianity and economics only indirectly and inferentially, another common method in academic circles shows how everything about Christianity directly concerns economics. Here a semantic relationship is drawn between what the two—theology and economics—are talking about. To make the whole discussion simpler and more concrete, let's narrow down the subject matters of theology and economics, on the one hand, to grace (by which I mean God's favor and all the ways God's favor is expressed—in creating the world, forgiving and remedying sin, offering spiritual and moral sanctification, and so on) and, on the other, to money (used as a short hand for material wealth and success and the like). Grace and money have everything to do with one another here, because from the viewpoint of Christianity the one means the other. Money means grace—it means one has grace; it is an indication of one's graced state. And grace means money—it means one has money; the grace one has, one's religious standing, is an indication of one's economic status. In short, the two have a direct semantic relationship as sign and meaning, signifier and signified.[4] One, it seems, is unpresentable and invisible, requiring the other to be its presentable and sensible replacement or substitute. Their relationship therefore involves at least implicitly some effort of hermeneutical decoding: one must ask, in other words, what grace or money, now taken as a sign, really means; understanding money or grace requires digging underneath it to its real and otherwise hidden significance.

Money Means Grace and Grace Means Money

Let's explore the one case a little further: money has everything to do with grace; money means grace. The history of Christian faith and practice is full of the search for signs of grace, money being just one of them. Grace is invisible, a spiritual and internal matter of the conversion of hearts and minds. Grace is as invisible as any of God's own acts that are unpresentable in their transcendence, in their difference from everything finite that can be pictured and imaged. To be sure of one's graced state therefore requires one to be assured by way of grace's signs. One's bodily state and bodily disciplines are often taken for such signs: the sweet odor of the saints, despite their refusal of all normal standards of hygiene; their incorruptible bodies despite the mortification of the flesh, despite the ascetic rigors to which they have been subjected, despite the length of time they have been in the grave. Control over the body and its insistent needs is taken, too, to be a sign of the workings of grace, a sign of one's spiritual virtuosity. Here it is the voluntary abnegation of wealth, voluntary poverty, among ascetics and monastic devotees that becomes a sign of grace.

Especially, however, with the birth of a state church in the age of Constantine, power, privilege, and success were often taken for such signs. Those in charge, those whom the fates of this world favor, are the chosen of God, God's lieutenants and servants. The emperor Constantine's victory over his rivals was an indication of his being favored by God; the church's victory over paganism by way of Constantine's rule was a sign of the grace that the church had been given. Indeed, the very wealth that once adorned pagan altars had been stripped from them, to be used for the building of churches. Here is the famous proof for Christianity from its spread—the success of Christianity as a world religion being the proof of the spirit and the power with which God has invested it.

Under this rubric, too, one finds success in one's calling as a sign of grace in Protestant, especially Calvinist, circles. The perennial need to know about one's graced state is here heightened by such things as the threat of a God who might as well damn to all eternity as save, by the inscrutability of God's decrees despite the revealed will of God to save in Christ, and by the loss of the reliability of the usual sacramental signs of grace in what is thought to be a corrupt church. Despite traditional worries about the corrupting influence of money, success in one's worldly calling steps into the breach. The elect of God are the very ones whose self-discipline and asceticism in worldly life make for economic success. The elect of God are able to adjust themselves to the disciplines of capitalist calculation at its beginnings; they become rich in a capitalist sense by saving, by amassing capital rather than spending. So the religious justification for a life of wealth and economic achievement is born and, along with it, the association of poverty with moral and spiritual degradation. Sociologists interested in the normative preconditions for capitalist forms of production and exchange—such as Max Weber—are, of course, happy to reproduce theological arguments of this sort, in which monetary success becomes the sign of grace, for their own descriptive and explanatory purposes.

Let's approach the matter from the other side now: grace has everything to do with money. Here divisions in the distribution of grace—religious differences most generally, differences in religious commitment, differences in religious affiliation—are taken to be signs of economic differences, for example, differences in class or status grouping. In this case (where grace is the sign rather than the signified), money and socio-political status are what cannot be mentioned. Or money and class are what should not be discussed in polite society or in the supposedly classless society of the United States, what, indeed, the veil of religion keeps from being mentioned as such. Grace is substituted for money, as money's representation, its representable stand-in or sign.

So, from a Marxist point of view, religious conflicts in the Reformation over the means of grace—over the number and significance of the sacraments, over faith or works as conditions of grace—become signs of economic and political conflict where a specifically economic and political vocabulary for engaging such conflicts is absent. People fight about religion at historical points where their real concerns for money and power cannot be raised directly or purely. Or, in cases where money and class can be mentioned but are being obfuscated, religious commitment and affiliation are simply part of the lifestyle markers for particular economic and social classes. So (depending on the time and place) an interest in the Church of England may mark you as a member of or aspirant to a particular social class, just as one's disinterest and failure to attend services mark you as a member of some other. Episcopalians, at one time at least, tended to be members of the U.S. "nobility"—membership in the Episcopal Church being one among a number of lifestyle and class markers, which included drinking and perhaps a certain tolerance of moral indiscretion. Evangelical groups, especially when they break away from a prior denomination, tend to be populated by those of lower economic and social status. And so on. Here the religious markers of class help to disguise the importance of economic and social differences by naturalizing them: What could be more natural than to be a member of the ruling class if one is an Episcopalian? The religious markers of class in this way help prevent or distract one from a more straightforwardly socio-economic and political analysis of the reasons for inequitable distributions of power and wealth in society. At least, such is the effect of religious markers of class before their demystification by a sociology of religion, which offers a hermeneutical key to their true interpretation and function. The specifically theological variant of this interpretation of religious affiliation as a signifier for money and class is found, for example, in H. Richard Niebuhr's *Social Sources of Denominationalism*: denominational divisions in the church universal, which match up with class, ethnic, and racial divides, are taken to be signs of corruption by nonreligious interests, by the forces of money and of racial and ethnic bias.[5]

The Dangers of a Semantic Analysis

Now these semantic readings of the relationship between grace and money—where either money or grace is sign or signifier—are all to the good in that they make clear the way religious concerns are bound up with those of an economic and socio-political nature. The semantic reading of those interrelations, however, forces a certain reductionism in the analysis—in two ways. First, the semantic framing of the relationship brings with it a simple correspondence between religious and economic statuses as the default mode of analysis. The potential differences between the two registers of grace and money are thereby concealed. For every grace there is its corresponding *equivalent* on the economic front (or the reverse): one searches for the matching sign for this particular signified, the matching signified for this particular sign. It is therefore presumed that members of the dominant religious faction are also members of the dominant economic class. Those who have economic goods—those with money—also have grace or religious goods, and vice versa. If you have cornered the market in material goods, you have also done so for spiritual ones. The successful are God's favored ones; God's favored ones become successful.

Second, by virtue of the semantic framing of the relationship, one or the other term—either grace or money, whichever one is viewed as the meaning of the other—is given an automatic explanatory privilege. Everything of significance in the one—the sign—is reduced to the other—its meaning. What is really at issue in worldly success is grace, or what is really at issue in one's religious standing is money. One is the appearance; the other is the reality. One is the epiphenomenon; the other the phenomenon. One is the superstructure; the other the base.

This second sort of reductionism, by the way, is often a feature of the method we discussed earlier for discussing the relationship between grace and money in functional terms. For example, reductionism appears in answering the question of how Calvinism's concern about the assurance of grace affects economic behavior by producing norms and dispositions that aid and abet a capitalist economy. This kind of relationship between grace and money defines one as the means and one as the end, and it always subordinates whatever is identified with the means, the end naturally being privileged over the means. So, for Max Weber, what is really of interest is to explain what gets people to conform their behavior to capitalist dictates. Religious beliefs and norms might have been important at the start, but now that capitalism has become an inescapable "iron cage," the subjective motivation, religious or otherwise, of economic actors drops out of the explanatory picture.[6] The capitalist machine—and therefore the sociologist interested in understanding it—does not care what your religion is. The functional equivalent of a religiously disciplined character, for example, is now the simple fear of starvation among workers who have no other way to support themselves.

The Pros and Cons of a Formal Analysis

A more complex and less presumptive way of framing the relationship involves a shift to a nonsemantic or formal mode of comparative analysis, like that found prototypically in structuralism (a shift that does not necessarily bring with it, as we'll see, the purely synchronic and politically naïve features that usually mar structuralism). What matters for comparative purposes is the internal organization of different systems; how the items within each system are related to one another establishes the basis for comparison, irrespective of the apparent meaning or reference of individual terms.[7] One doesn't ask, then, what grace means, as if it doesn't mean what it appears to mean, being a sign of something else. One doesn't have to ask this because the connection between grace and money is simply not established semantically, by showing that the one means the other. An account of the relationship between the two is developed instead by attending to the respective ways that grace and money are organized or distributed in human life; the two can be compared along those lines—they belong in the same universe of discourse—even if the meanings or references of the terms have nothing to do with one another.

Whatever grace means—and it may mean nothing like what money means—a connection can still be established between them by looking at the organizational or structural features of the two relatively autonomous arenas or areas of life in which they figure. One compares the ways grace and money are placed within the differential networks or fields constituted by their respective principles of distribution. In short, one compares the system of exchanges, substitutions, and circulations that hold for grace and for money, respectively, without having to presume, substantively, that money and grace are at all alike. One simply asks, for example, how is grace distributed? Is it distributed the way money is distributed? And how might the two forms of distribution intersect in particular times and places, by way of structural or formal parallels between the two?

For a simple case of such an intersection between the relatively autonomous fields or networks established by grace and money respectively, take the way a religious worldview—say, a Protestant rejection of institutionally mediated forms of grace—arises in response (at least in part) to specifically religious needs and anxieties and then enters into a primarily economically determined distribution of statuses. It enters into that economic sphere by way of an elective affinity between certain structural elements of that religious worldview and a lifestyle associated with a particular economic status. For example, independent entrepreneurs making up the new merchant class in early modern Europe feel themselves to be on their own economically the way Protestants are on their own religiously; that is the sort of formal affinity to be found here between the relatively autonomous fields of grace and economic status. By virtue of such an elective affinity, the members of this status group become the carriers of such a religious worldview—its primary adherents—and thereby alter the development of that religious perspective so as to bring about greater conformity between it and the interests and needs of this particular class. This is at a minimum the sort of complex analysis that would replace a simple semantic framing of the relationship between money and grace. It is Weberian in character.[8]

The categories used to frame such a formal or structural comparison between grace and money are crucial. In comparative frameworks influenced by structuralism (that of Claude Levi-Strauss in particular), the categories enabling formal comparison among all the fields of human life (cultural, social, economic, religious, and so forth)— categories of exchange, distribution, transformation, substitution— are derived primarily from linguistics, and from a very peculiar form of linguistics at that. Structural linguistics is a form of linguistics that stresses static, already established linguistic systems, rather than asking about the complex, conflict-laden processes by which a linguistic system (like standard English) comes to be established. Structuralism also isolates such systems from their actual uses in politically and economically charged situations. Using the categories of structural linguistics therefore has the effect of de-politicizing the framing categories for comparison, and the comparisons themselves are taken out of any conflict-ridden, politically and economically charged space.

To remedy these defects, sociologists and anthropologists like Pierre Bourdieu, who is a follower of Max Weber in this regard, substitute economic categories for linguistic ones, or give those linguistic categories an economic spin.[9] One can place religion and money in the same analytic space or frame by talking of religious interests and investments, and attempts to monopolize grace (as Weber already did); one can talk of specifically religious forms of capital. Every field or arena of life is defined by some sort of good or value specific to it; every field establishes the value of a particular sort of good, in which all the participants in the field have an investment or they wouldn't be participating in it. In the case of Christianity, let's say the good or value that defines the field is salvation. All the participants in the field are after that good or value; those are the stakes of the game. The field amounts, therefore, to the establishment of a market in that sort of good or value. The participants are distributed differently, located differently in the space of the field by their abilities to gain it, by their capital—by whatever it is, specific to this field, that enables one to achieve the goods of the field. In the Christian case, grace and the means to grace would constitute these field-specific resources or capital.

The two forms of reductionism I mentioned in the case of semantic accounts of the relationship between grace and money resurface here, however; and bring with them a tendency to prejudge the degree to which an economy of grace can differ from others.

On the face of it, the first form of reductionism—the presumption of a simple correspondence or match between the two, between grace and money—seems to be avoided. For a number of reasons, in Bourdieu's understanding of things it no longer makes sense to *assume*, for example, that those who occupy a dominant position in the religious field correspond to those with a dominant position in the economic or political field—to assume, say, that members of the established national church are always members of the establishment, the power structures of society. It does not make sense to assume this, first of all, because one never understands a position in one field by immediately mapping it onto a position in another. A position in a field is to be understood, first, with reference to its differences from other positions in the same field; comparing positions across fields is therefore always a matter of comparing relations between positions in one field to relations between positions in another. At most, Bourdieu is on the lookout, then, for structural analogies or homologies across fields where relations between positions in one field reflect relations between positions in another. For example, golf is to professional wrestling in the field of sports what doctors and lawyers are to factory workers in the field of economic employment; therefore hitting the tees conveys white collar distinction, while yelling for blood at a World Wrestling Federation match is a marker of blue-collar style. Nothing is explained by simply saying that golf represents a high economic standing, unless one understands the way golf differs from other games in the field of sports. The high cost of equipment and greens fees, which might suggest a direct connection with economic status, isn't so much at issue here; more important are the purely sporting ways, so to speak, that golf differs from other games—by not being a team sport, by using clubs that are a long way from the ball, by play that avoids all violence and even physical contact with others and that requires an unusual degree of bodily precision and emotional control. These distinctive features of golf compared with other sports are what form an analogy with the distance from economic necessity that distinguishes a high economic class from a low one.

A position in one field never simply reflects, then, a position in another field; the connection with that second field is always instead refracted through the field-specific forms of difference that constitute the first one. For example, a literary work of high art may ultimately make a lot of money for its author—status in the literary field corresponding then with economic status. But in order to be a work of high art and not lowbrow, a literary work must repudiate all immediate profits to be made from meeting the popular tastes of a mass market. It will therefore make money—and probably quite a bit more than some cheap pulp romance—only once it is deemed a literary classic and assigned widely in school curricula. Literary status can be correlated with economic status, then, only by passing through, or by being refracted by the way differences between high and low art are established in the literary field.

Because relations rather than positions are brought into correspondence, there is, moreover, always a certain flexibility to the way homologies may be drawn. The difference between high and low culture, for example, can map onto the difference between fractions of the dominant class; the difference between high and low culture will therefore become a marker of the difference between those who make their money by way of educational credentials (such as professors) and those who make it through business expertise. Or it can be mapped onto the difference between the whole of that dominant class and the underclasses; the underclasses are the ones with lowbrow tastes, enjoying Broadway theatre and never bothering with difficult, off-Broadway productions. Or the same cultural distinctions can be used to align cultural elites with the underclasses against businessmen, since the former share the position of dominated in different fields of power, in the one case within the dominant class, in the other between it and the whole rest of the social field.

For Bourdieu, whether spiritual or religious capital lines up with economic capital is also a historically contingent matter of the conversion or exchange rates between fields. For example, in some times and places—say, medieval Europe—religious prestige will bring with it economic wealth; the one can be converted into the other. At other times and places—say, the contemporary United States—that is not so certain.

Finally, dominance in one field does not necessarily conform to dominance in another because sometimes high standing in one field is defined over and against the criteria that determine value in another. For example, a work of art will lose standing in aesthetic terms if it is produced to make money by catering to popular tastes; one has to repudiate economic motives in order to have high standing in the artistic field. Weber suggested indeed that the same sort of thing went for religions of salvation such as Christianity: the distinctive good offered by Christianity is defined over and against the usual forms of capital that one might amass in this life. Rather than dominance in the religious field directly matching up as a matter of course with dominance in the economic, social, and political fields, religious investments are, as often as not, out of sync with one's economic or political capital.

Specifically religious interests in salvation, Weber argues, take their start at least from dissatisfaction with the distributions of other sorts of goods—from the sense that a society's norms for economic and political distribution are not reflected in the realities of social life or from worries, in any case, about the justice and meaning of inequalities in the social and economic distribution of goods. Because of this dynamic, the massing of religious capital is often compensatory, making up for the lack of capital on the economic, social, or political fronts. People in the lower classes of society do not adhere to a religion that immediately reflects their social status. They are attracted to a religious perspective that offers them a form of religious capital at variance with the quality or quantity of capital they have in other spheres. For example, they are attracted to evangelical forms of Christianity (say, Baptist congregations or Methodism in its early days) in which the distribution of grace, by way of the workings of the Spirit, floats free of and therefore fails to correspond to the social distribution of wealth.

Bourdieu's interest in homologies or structural parallels across fields has the tendency, however, to support a sort of historicist assumption—the assumption, in other words, that all the fields (religious, economic, and so forth) in a particular historical period share a similar structure and are organized as fields according to the same basic principles. For all the complexities, this assumption always enables a simple one-to-one correspondence to be drawn among positions across different fields; the fields at any one time and place always seem to mirror one another in their basic structure.

A very interesting case of such a historicist assumption is found in the work of Jean-Joseph Goux, who constructs a general theory of stages of symbolization to make sense of what logocentrism, phallocentrism, monotheism, and the dominance of the money medium have in common:[10] the construction of what Goux, following Marx, calls a general equivalent of value. Comparing the values of materially quite different things, whether that comparison be conceptual, religious, or economic, requires the creation of a norm for value more abstract than anything subject to comparison. Take the case of simple barter: I'll make you dinner if you cut my hair. Implicit in the transaction is the appeal to some notion of value more abstract than the value of the meal or the hair-cutting, which establishes the equivalence of the exchange. The development of currency, of money, makes this appeal to some more abstract notion of value explicit and regularizes transactions by way of a single agreed-upon standard or norm of value. The wider the field of comparison (that is, the more disparate the work that this norm for value performs), the more abstract the norm for value becomes until it is the general equivalent for anything and everything in the field subject to comparative evaluation. The general equivalent can now replace or be the stand-in for anything in the field, at the same time as it tends to be projected out of the field as a whole as the transcendent, supreme value ordering and directing every exchange beneath it and serving as the guarantee for any value achieved by way of those transactions.

The various historical stages in this symbolization process are constituted by a correspondence in the form and function of the abstract norm for value across a variety of fields. For example, at the last historical stage mentioned (there are others to come too), God in the religious field corresponds to the gold standard of the economic sphere. God is the supreme value locked away from the sphere of this-worldly transaction in some heavenly Fort Knox of transcendence, the supreme value into which everything in the world, if it is genuinely to be valuable, must ultimately be convertible: God, like the gold standard, must stand behind it as its value in hard cash. In much earlier economic periods, the God of an iconoclastic monotheism would fail to appear or intervene in the representable, material transactions of everyday life just as money fails to appear or intervene as the facilitator of economic exchange in a primarily barter economy—where money is used to evaluate the worth of what is exchanged but does not itself change hands in the transactions.

Goux recognizes that the stages of symbolization of the general equivalent need not occur at the same time in the different spheres of religion, economy, and philosophy, but clearly a correspondence among the various fields is assumed as the historical baseline. An idea of God that does not correspond to the stage that the general equivalent has reached in the economy is either an anachronism (a remnant of a historically superceded stage of symbolization) or utopian (a mere idea without any correspondence to the realities of economic fact).

Weber and Bourdieu are able to avoid this totalizing of historical periods, in which the same structural features are thought to recur in all the fields of society, because they see society and historical periods not as wholes but as made up of competing status groups and classes. And that is indeed typical of their position, in contrast to the functionalism of, say, Émile Durkheim, in which the explanatory stress is always on the way social and cultural forms make for social cohesion and integration. But Bourdieu does incorporate Durkheim's viewpoint in his account of the habitus: the habitus or fundamental forms of classification literally embodied below the level of explicit consciousness in people's tastes and in the ways they are naturally inclined to act, internalize the fundamental divisions of the whole social structure, ultimately between dominated and dominant.[11] The fundamental oppositions or principles of division that make up those forms of classification are therefore shared by all members of society and will reappear (with field-specific variations) as a kind of commonsense baseline for the organization of all the fields in a society. Every field is therefore basically organized in the same way, and this guarantees homologies across the fields, a kind of pre-established harmony among them, in which one can always locate the relatively equivalent position in one field for a position in another.

The second kind of reductionism I mentioned above is an even more serious problem. Bourdieu is commonly charged, indeed, with reducing other fields to the economic and thereby overlooking what makes them distinctive by talking about them all in overly narrow, economic terms. The members of every field, it is charged, are turned into purely self-concerned calculators of what will most benefit them economically. The way rational-choice theorists talk, say, about the cost/benefit assessment of economic utilities is turned into a human universal and superimposed on every kind of human enterprise in every time and place. The focus is always on the way individuals try to maximize what serves their own self-interests under conditions of constraint and scarcity.

Before we are convinced too quickly by this criticism, however, it is important to be fair to Bourdieu and to see how his economic framing of a comparison between fields is precisely designed to avoid this sort of economic reductionism.[12] Making the economy (in a narrow sense) a field is, first of all, incompatible with the usual rational-choice understanding of economic action. Bourdieu is therefore in fact rejecting what he is thought to be reducing everything to.

Bourdieu's account of fields is, for example, incompatible with the usual methodological individualism of modern economic theories. People do not come together as independent individuals for the sake of better satisfying their material needs and what results is a social system of trade; they act the way they do—they trade—because they are already social actors, because they have internalized the social structures of exchange that constitute that economic field. And what they are after, the goods to be gained through participation in a particular form of economy—say, the good of maximum personal profit—are not human universals, but the historically conditioned products of that particular field. Maximum profit isn't anything that people want, for example, apart from their inclusion in a capitalist field that first developed only after the eighteenth century in most parts of Europe. The very propensity to calculate costs and benefits in a deliberate fashion is, moreover, the product of a certain sort of adjustment to one's social environment—for all its conscious character it is still rooted in a bodily based habitus in Bourdieu's sense—and therefore this propensity has socio-historical conditions usually ignored by rational-choice theorists. Bourdieu believes, indeed, that the poor and marginalized in capitalist societies are routinely deprived of control over their lives in ways that socialize them against planning ahead; they lack the social prerequisites for the very sort of rational calculation that economists think everyone naturally engages in.[13] To the extent rational-choice theorists are right about the economic field, narrowly construed, they are then describing something that is highly historically circumscribed and of very limited social reach. Clearly Bourdieu can have no intention of attributing this sort of thing to every field.

When Bourdieu extends the economic to all fields, he is countering the monopoly that rational choice theory gives to the economic in a narrow sense; making all fields economic in a general sense is just to say that there are forms of economy that cannot be reduced to a simple self-interested deliberation about the relative utilities of different courses of action.[14] If economics in the restricted sense specified by rational choice theory is the only form of economic field, then the fields of religion or art must be relegated to the noneconomic, which generally means, from an economic point of view, to the sphere of personal values rather than institutional structures, to the realm of mere culture and of irrational feelings or passions, and to a simple concern for the other-worldly or the ethereal. Pushed out of economy, those fields pose no challenge to the narrow way that the economic is understood; self-interested calculation might very well exhaust its meaning.

Once other fields are understood in Bourdieu's economic terms, the sense of the economic is necessarily broadened beyond anything rational-choice theorists would affirm. Even fields that are structured in ways that discourage overtly self-interested calculation of material benefit exhibit an economy, and therefore the economic "calculation" that spans fields must be at bottom more a matter of feel or unconscious tact than conscious deliberation. This suggests, indeed, that in all fields—even a modern capitalist economy—one's self-interest is not served primarily through calculation of costs and benefits but by an inarticulate feel for what makes the best sense for oneself, given the state of play of the game and one's accumulated capital. This is, for example, how people tend to replicate their parents' social class in choosing their line of work—by simply doing what comes naturally without much forethought, in the way they have been socialized.

In some fields, moreover, material well-being is ensured by the very opposite of the behaviors a rational-choice theorist would advise; the economists' restricted sense of economic rationality is thereby exploded. In these societies, it does not make much economic sense to try directly to maximize one's wealth or make material gain one's overt concern. In societies like the ones Bourdieu studied in Algeria, one can ensure one's material well-being only if one has a good reputation, and one only has that by giving one's goods away to others with what looks like a total lack of self-concern. The primary "products" of such an economy are not the discrete material objects of exchange that rational choice theory fixates on but the social relations in which all parties are embedded. People are heavily invested in the character of these social relations; their lives revolve around the ups and downs of their relative social standing. But investment here does not take a monetary form and therefore the sense of investment used for comparative purposes loses any narrow economic register; it broadens to include a willingness to expend time, energy, and resources, in a potentially immeasurable manner, on the pursuit of these goods established by the field. Here the means/ends calculations that come to the fore in a capitalist economy might very well be subordinated to the absolute value-orientations, as Weber would call them, of tradition and religion without jeopardizing in the least the field's economic form: this is the way the well-being of the community has always been assured, or this is the way that God wants it, and that's that, whatever the potential costs from a rational-choice theorist's point of view ("if only they didn't destroy all those blankets in ceremonial potlatches, they might all be a bit warmer in the winter!").

But the primary way Bourdieu avoids reductionism is by allowing each field to define its own distinctive interests and ends; those distinctive interests and goals are what make the fields at least relatively autonomous from one another, for all their complex exchange relations and correspondences. The religious field, for example, is not defined by an interest in money or wealth but by an interest in salvation and in the means to getting it—grace. Bourdieu is fond of giving a particular example in reply to the charge of reductionism: The artistic field is not defined by an interest in money but, if anything, by an interest in being disinterested in money. If everything you do as an artist is very obviously geared to economic profit, your work is unlikely for that very reason to meet any of the field-specific criteria for great art, and you'll fall under the suspicion of being no "real" artist at all. In a similar fashion, if your agenda as a religious leader is to have a nice house and car from the donations of your followers, you are unlikely to be classified a saint. Indeed, the more that the distinctively religious or artistic values of a field become blurred across the board with economic ones, the less there is any religious or artistic field to speak of.

Bourdieu does, however, make other assumptions about what is required for a field—assumptions about field invariants—that have reductive implications.[15] You don't have a field unless the distinctive good of the field can be made rare and scarce, turned into a kind of exclusive privilege from which others are shut out; you don't have a field unless the good of that field is something that can be distributed unequally and that is potentially subject to exclusive appropriation. A field is defined as a structured space of positions where those positions are determined by differences (of volume or quality) in the distribution of the resources or capital typical of the field. If the good of the field isn't rare, if you can't exclude others from it, and if that good isn't distributed unevenly in fact among the participants, there is nothing to fight over, and those fights are just what all the jockeying for position in a field is all about; every field is determined by contests among its participants that aim to maintain or transform the uneven distribution of capital that presently organizes it.

The relative autonomy among the interests of various fields does not mean, then, that there isn't a competition within each and every field for distinction in accordance with its particular field-specific value. Bourdieu fully expects, for example, a competition for status by way of the achievement of disinterestedness to characterize the artistic field. The relative autonomy of the interests of different fields simply does not extend to the character of their markets. Whatever the interests of the field, the market set up is always like a competitive monetary market. Whatever the field, one is always trying to maximize one's capital, dominate the market in the good at issue, and achieve distinction through an ideally exclusive possession of that good, over and against one's competitors in the field. Grace, then, like disinterestedness in the artistic field, would have to circulate like money.

This sort of reduction of the markets of all fields to a very narrowly framed economic market is what is ultimately behind the first form of reductionism we talked about. The positions of every field will necessarily and automatically map onto those of the economy, in a narrow sense, because every field must be structured fundamentally according to the contrasts found there—ultimately between dominant and dominated. Because the markets of all fields must be similar to a competitive monetary market, the goods of every field, even those that have nothing to do with money, are always available to reinforce economic distinctions by lining up with them. In every field, there is always a distinction between high and low, between those who exhibit the values or have the goods of the field in sufficient quantity or quality and those who don't—suitable for mapping onto those with and without capital in the economic field. It is in this way that cultural fields serve to legitimate economic differences—by naturalizing them. Those who make up the dominant economic classes are just the sort of people to appreciate the exquisite abstractness of a painting by Rothko, whose rarity is attested by the guard who keeps watch over it in the Museum of Modern Art, while working-class people fancy paintings of Elvis on velvet sold to any passerby in gas station parking lots, and lower-middle-class artistic sensibilities run to copies of pretty pictures by "old masters," mass-produced in Asia and destined for the decoration of living rooms across America. What could be more natural than to be in the upper economic echelons if one is a person with such refined aesthetic tastes? One's exceptional personal qualities serve both to make sense of and to legitimize one's economic standing. The jobs that make for an upper-class life are obviously not for those with common tastes!

The Potential for Noncompetitiveness

Now in charging Bourdieu's economic framing of the comparison between grace and money with reductionism I would hate to lose what is valuable about it. One of Bourdieu's intents here is clearly to avoid the over-idealization of intellectual and cultural fields. He is trying to get away from the idea that those fields are somehow above it all, above being embroiled in the sort of fights over power and status that are so obvious in the economic and political arenas of life. One can retain this valuable insight along with Bourdieu's basic framework. What one must not do, however, is use it to exclude the possibility that some fields are working to establish noncompetitive forms of circulation. What is most interesting about the distribution of grace, it seems to me, is just this proposal of a non-monetary, anti-monetary (because noncompetitive) market in goods.

If the field of grace is determined, as every field is, by a fight, it is primarily a fight between those favoring noncompetitive forms of exchange, on the one hand, and those trying to institute the competitive forms characteristic of other fields, on the other. Bourdieu recognizes that the fundamental way the goods of a field are defined is one of the things at issue in the contests that make it up—not just how people or products are positioned relative to the goods and values that everyone in a field agrees upon.[16] For example, under dispute in artistic fields is not just who at any particular moment best exhibits the values of pure art for art's sake but the degree to which values must be purified in this way of all other motives, of, say, crass materialism, in order to be artistic. Artistic fields typically include a fight between purveyors of high art and more commercial artists over how a legitimate work of art is to be defined. Bourdieu just refuses to see that contests of this sort could go on at an even more fundamental level—that the contests could concern whether the goods of the field are to be matters for competitive struggle or not.

By focusing exclusively on a competitive market in grace, neither Weber nor Bourdieu is able to pick up on this possibility of a struggle toward a noncompetitively defined religious field. Observe, for example, how Weber and Bourdieu discuss controversies over the means of grace between clerics and charismatic religious virtuosos.[17] The religious virtuoso does an end run around the cleric by claiming the status of graced person through an institutionally unmediated relationship with God—a relationship that does not come by way of official role or educational certification. This achievement is a rare one, distinguishing the religious virtuoso from all other believers, who, as Friedrich Schleiermacher would say, are mere believers at second hand.[18] The cleric offers to all these others a kind of democratization of grace: nothing is difficult here; all you have to do is come to church. And in the process the cleric solidifies the clerical monopoly on the means of grace: everybody can get grace but only at the hands of a priest. The religious virtuoso can, however, make his or her own appeal to all those whom the clerical hierarchy disadvantages, to the masses of religious people whose status is low in institutional and educational terms, whether in or outside of church. Whatever one's position in institutionalized hierarchies of whatever kind, one can achieve the very highest status in religious terms through the way modeled for you by the religious virtuoso. The hierarchies that disadvantage you are corrupt; you have a worthiness in the eyes of God as great as any priest; God has a special regard and mission for those who are lowly in the eyes of the world; one's true status will become clear in the future or after death. By way of this sort of appeal, the religious virtuoso might, indeed, achieve the highest religious status as the founder of a new religious movement.

Overlooked in this account of struggles for status by way of struggles over the means of grace is something I think the historical record also makes quite clear: for all the status warfare, one thing that the oppressed are looking for and are attracted to in religion is a way out of the competitive circulation of goods. They hope not for a status to rival the great but for a circulation of goods without status rivalry. What attracts the oppressed is a vision of a grace offered to all without regard for distinctions of status: the lowly in the eyes of the world or in the eyes of the institutionalized church can have it just as well as the privileged can. This grace is offered freely to all; to be favored by God with it one does not have to be learned or wealthy or socially well-connected or male or white. So Donald Mathews describes religion in the Old South: "'God is no respecter of persons' (Acts 10:34) was one of the most popular biblical passages in black Christianity, cropping up as it did in sermons, conversations, reminiscences, and confrontations with white people."[19]

In the distribution of grace, distinctions of status make no difference. In the first place, certainly, they make no difference because the distribution of grace does not follow the lines of already established differences of status. But in the second place they are irrelevant because the distribution of grace need not itself produce or foster any new competitive markets in status. The distribution of grace need not, in other words, establish simply an alternative competition for status, with new standards to replace the old, discriminating between high and low now, not on the basis of economic achievement or social standing, but with reference to one's holiness or the genuineness of one's conversion experience. Nor need grace be merely an alternative means to elevation in the eyes of the world, a way of aspiring to a higher social class through the proposal of a new form of capital. Although it happens frequently enough, there is no necessity to the fact that, as H. Richard Niebuhr elegantly expresses it, "the history of denominationalism reveals itself as the history of the religiously neglected poor, who fashion a new type of Christianity which corresponds to their distinctive needs, who rise in the economic scale under the influence of religious discipline, and who, in the midst of a freshly acquired cultural respectability, neglect the new poor succeeding them on the lower plane."[20] Running contrary to this dynamic, grace is often thought to be always directed especially to the lowly in order to raise all to a common height.

In these regards, the religions of the oppressed are true to, are the saviors and keepers of, a neglected strand of thinking present in Christianity from the very beginning. In this way of looking at things, what is notable about Christianity as a field, what is unusual about it, is its attempt to institute a circulation of goods to be possessed by all in the same fullness of degree without diminution or loss, a distribution that in its prodigal promiscuity calls forth neither the pride of superior position nor rivalrous envy among its recipients. Breaking this down into its various elements: The good is distributed by God and is to be distributed by us in imitation of God, in an indiscriminate, profligate fashion that fails to reflect the differences in worthiness and status that rule the arrangements of a sinful world. The purpose of the giving is elevation, without limit, so as to bring all recipients to the level of the giver, ultimately God. The whole is given to each or at the very least is continually being offered to each, awaiting the expansion of the recipients' capacity to receive the whole, which God and the followers of God are also trying to bring about. The good is distributed without the giver suffering any loss thereby. The recipients of such gifts do not amass them in a static way, as goods simply to be kept, but become givers in turn. The recipients do not hold the good simply for themselves, as a form of exclusive possession. There is no point to any of that, since one is more oneself and more perfectly oneself in giving to others. The reception of the good by others increases or confirms (in the case of God) the giver's own goodness.

These unusual characteristics of Christianity as a field are, I think, one reason for the appeal of Platonism at Christianity's start; Christianity (along with some forms of Neoplatonism) selects for aspects of Platonism like these. The heavens for Plato form a realm of harmony, without jealousy or strife. In Plato's myth of the winged soul's fall, the soul aspires to "the heavens . . . where the blessed gods pass to and fro, each doing his or her own work, and within them are all such as will and can follow them, for Jealousy has no place in the choir divine. . . . Such is the life of the gods. . . . As for the rest, though all are eager to reach the heights and seek to follow they are not able; sucked down as they travel they trample and tread on one another, this one striving to outstrip that. Thus, confusion ensues and conflict and grievous sweat."[21] The creator of the world, again according to Plato (in the *Timaeus* this time), creates the world according to the model of this divine world—without jealousy: "[The creator of the world] was good and the good cannot be jealous of anything. And being free of jealousy, the creator desired that all things should be as like himself as possible."[22] Without jealousy are those who imitate the gods, the teachers and students, lovers and beloveds of this world at its best, according to Plato, each of whom is to be made like the gods through the mutually elevating influences of every other. Plato in the *Phaedrus* proposes a paradigm of reciprocal benefit in loving: whatever good the lover draws from the gods, who offer the good without jealousy, is to be poured out onto the beloved, so that as one is drawn up to the gods, so also is the other.

This affirmation of giving out of one's own fullness and without loss to those in need, for the very purpose of making them "rivals" in one's own gifts, can be found everywhere in Christianity, if one is looking for it. It is evident in all the topics of Christian theology, at least as a submerged theme—in the account of trinitarian relations, God's creation of the world, God's presence in the world, God's distribution of all the goods of grace from creation to salvation, and our responsibilities to others. The whole Christian story, from top to bottom, can be viewed as an account of the production of value and the distribution of goods, following this peculiar noncompetitive shape.

It can be found throughout the whole history of Christian thought in the most unexpected places, perhaps—from Dionysius the Areopagite through Thomas Aquinas to Martin Luther, to name just a few. It is the love of the hierarch in Dionysius that gives for the benefit of subordinates, so that they too may receive the very same benefit. It is the faith and love, for Luther, "by which a human being is placed between God and her neighbor as a medium which receives from above and gives out again below, and is like a vessel or tube through which the stream of divine blessings must flow without intermission to other people."[23] It is the dynamic character of the world for Thomas Aquinas, in which one perfects oneself in imitation of the self-diffusing goodness of God by perfecting others. It is the love of paradise that is the counter to the seven deadly sins as Dante presents them—sins of pride and of envy in particular in which one holds what one has against one's needy neighbors or begrudges them what they have of the good out of anxious self-concern.

This is a fullness of giving without gradual depletion or loss like that of the sun, one of the most common images for God in the Christian tradition, the sun that remains resplendent however much it illuminates others and that only gets brighter as the light it shines on everything is reflected back onto it. Rather than being achieved at the expense of others or given out at one's own expense, here light feeds light, joy feeds joy, delight feeds delight. Dante again: "The infinite and inexpressible Grace . . . gives itself to Love as a sunbeam gives itself to a bright surface. As much light as it finds there, it bestows; thus as the blaze of Love is spread more widely, the greater the Eternal Glory grows. As mirror reflects mirror, so above, the more there are who join their souls, the more Love learns perfection, and the more they love."[24]

On this vision of things the whole of God's goodness is distributed to each, in the way that, as Plotinus, that non-Christian so dear to many in the early church, says, the soul is present entire to every part of the body, or the whole vital principle of a tree, and not merely some portion of it, is to be found in each leaf. Without a speck of jealousy or pride in its own possession, God is always offering the whole of the good to everyone, limited only by our capacities to receive, limitations that may be the product of natural forms of finitude or of a divinely arranged diversity of roles in church or society, but are more likely the result of our own sinful institution of contrary, competitive economies. Wherever possible, those who are offered the whole of the good by God are to pass on what they receive in that same fashion—with the demand for equality of distribution.

Even natural limitations that account for diversity in the reception of the whole good offered are subject to indefinite expansion via the workings of grace—something that Origen and Gregory of Nyssa in the early church, for example, affirm quite strongly (at least for people, in Gregory's case). All things in the world, whatever their differences in kind, might be elevated to the level of the highest good, for example, in a communion or union with God's own goodness that would make that goodness one's own without loss of one's particular nature. Inequalities that remain among creatures who retain the particularities of their identities are, ideally, not a matter of rank but a matter simply of a diversity of genuine goods.

An Economically Irrelevant Pipe Dream?

As my high-flown rhetoric at points might suggest, it is easy to think of this noncompetitive economy as a pipe dream, deferred until the utopian space of heaven. The references to Platonism don't help, suggesting that this noncompetitive economy can be instituted only for spiritual goods, in a realm of grace divorced from the material world, from the everyday fields of economics and politics. One might think only joy or knowledge is subject to noncompetitive distribution—nothing that is physically embodied. For example, some piece of knowledge can be shared equally by any number of knowers in a noncompetitive fashion; my knowledge increases your knowledge, and yours, in turn, mine. But can the same thing be true for a car or a house? This sort of Platonic dualism between material and spiritual is often, of course, incorporated into Christianity along with the ideals of a noncompetitive economy. H. Richard Niebuhr, as late as 1929, wrote, "The values to which [the modern world] gives the greatest veneration and which it pursues with greatest abandon are values which inherently lead to strife and conflict. They are political and economic goods which cannot be shared without diminution and which arouse cupidity and strife rather than lead to cooperation and peace."[25]

But (pace Niebuhr) the Christian tradition—at least this quite common, albeit often overlooked variant of the Christian tradition I'm developing—affirms at a minimum that God creates the whole world, in all its aspects—material and spiritual—according to such a noncompetitive economy, so that it should be such a noncompetitive economy to every degree possible; it holds us as creatures of body and soul up to its measure. The social worlds of economics and politics as we find them certainly do not run according to principles of a noncompetitive economy, but as modern people we are aware of their malleability by our own efforts, the way such structures are maintained only by way of our own complicity with them. By setting Christian ideas of the production and circulation of goods into a comparative economy, by making that comparative framing an economic one, my intent is just to suggest that a Christian economy has everything to do with the material dimensions of life—with the economic more narrowly construed. It is clear that, set within a comparative economy, grace has everything to do with money. By avoiding all forms of reductionism in that economic framing of the comparison, I am trying to allow grace its distinctive voice. Grace has everything to do with money because in grace money finds its greatest challenger and most obstreperous critic.

2

IMAGINING ALTERNATIVES
TO THE PRESENT ECONOMIC SYSTEM

The last chapter showed how the same general economic frame of analysis could be used to discuss both theology and economics (in a narrow sense), without prejudicing the degree to which a theological economy might differ from what we ordinarily think of as economy. The basic story that Christians tell directly concerns economic issues and offers a systematic vision of how economic life should be ordered. Given this way of looking at it, one can bring the Christian story into direct conversation with all sorts of other economic views.

The last chapter also began to sketch some of the unusual principles of a theological economy, in which, for example, goods circulate both without self-sacrifice and for the benefit of others. In this chapter I develop such principles further and more systematically, by throwing them into the mix of a number of other understandings of economy. The meaning of the principles of a theological economy becomes clearer when unpacked with reference to these contrasting forms.

I already suggested in the last chapter that what makes a theological economy odd is its capacity to violate the usual strictures of a competitive monetary market. Now I wish to compare the basic principles of a theological economy with those of a capitalist economy, particularly capitalism's underlying assumptions about property and possession.

Theological Economy's Response to Capitalism

The comparison will prove illuminating. When theological economy is brought into conversation with capitalism, the usual assumptions about alternatives to capitalism, for example, are skewed. A primary economic question becomes, for example, not simply who owns (that is, the question of private or state ownership), but the very meaning of possession at a much more fundamental level.

The comparison with capitalism here is not just an expository device; to a certain extent the comparison is what helps me formulate the principles of theological economy to begin with. I am not, then, simply bringing into conversation already constituted fields, after the fact. The fields of theology and economy (in a narrow sense) may be relatively autonomous in that their respective interests and markets are nothing alike, but that doesn't mean they come to be constructed independently of one another. As I wrote in the preface, theological ideas originate in the effort to set them off against those of the wider society. I am engaged in just this sort of effort now.

The Christian story of economy that I tell is not, then, simply found. As evidenced by its variability over the course of a complex two-thousand-year history, the Christian story about God, creation, providence, and salvation is a highly malleable story, susceptible to multiple readings of the notions at issue and multiple accounts of how these notions are all to be tied together coherently. The way I tell the story—while deeply informed by the history of Christian thought and by an appreciation for what is theologically at stake—is specifically designed, nonetheless, to be capitalism's contrast case.

Theology in this way becomes part of a wider effort by scholars in a number of different academic disciplines to free up space in which to imagine alternatives to capitalism—at least to its present configuration in which so many nations, and so much of the population of every one, wallow in poverty and despair. The economic options of history seem to have come to an end, to have narrowed to this final one. With the demise of Eastern European and Soviet-style communism and the introduction into China of capitalist economic principles, there seems no alternative to capitalism. It is capitalism or nothing—capitalism as presently organized or nothing. Experiments with social welfare states in the West have faltered; efforts by individual nations to stem the flow of capitalism's rush to spots with cheaper labor or sounder currencies seem flattened by the free-market juggernaut. It is the free-wheeling capitalism of today or nothing. Although as modern people we know that we are responsible for the shape of the societies we live in and that society's structures can be modified by human means, we have no idea of what we might replace the present system with, no vision of a different system to spur revision of the present one's inhumanities. Our ability to imagine alternative economic structures is constricted and constrained.

The discipline of theology in a time of economic dead ends can work to open up the economic imagination in much the way the disciplines of history and anthropology can; it can fund socio-cultural criticism in the way that histories of political and economic ideas, and cultural anthropology do.[1] History reveals the variability and flexibility of even those economic ideas with which capitalism has been allied. Anthropology undercuts the inevitability of our economic understanding from the outside, so to speak; viable economic forms cannot be limited to those of our past and present.

This chapter takes up two such alternative economies offered by the history of political and economic thought in the West and by anthropology, respectively. One stems from an interpretation of the writings of John Locke, the other from the anthropological literature on noncommodity gift exchange in South Asia. Both center around ideas of inalienable property, or property that, while circulating, remains in some sense common or shared. Like what happened with the case of capitalism, but now in more a positive fashion, my ideas of theological economy will be developed in light of these two alternatives. Neither seems capitalistic in its underlying assumptions. Both have resonances with Christian theology. The first case, that of Locke, is itself a theological vision of sorts, and the basic principles at work in it have had a great deal of influence on theology, both before and after him. The other example—the sort of noncommodity gift exchanges of interest to anthropologists since Bronislaw Malinowski and Marcel Mauss—are presently quite influential in a number of theological circles, for example, in the work of John Milbank and Radical Orthodoxy. Might these economies of inalienable property help point the way beyond capitalism to a distinctively different theological economy of grace?

I will be sketching the principles of capitalism as a foil, then, for my own proposals. And these historical and anthropological cases will be mined for some sense of what it would take to move beyond those capitalist principles. In those ways, I hope to develop a theological alternative to capitalism of the strongest sort, one that escapes the stale and hackneyed contrast between communism and capitalism or even between socialism and capitalism. Such contrasts have in any case become outmoded with the present worldwide loss of confidence in both government ownership of major industries and central planning in resource allocation. One can move beyond socialist compromise to fierce antagonism directed at capitalism in principle; but communism need not exhaust the understanding of what that might mean.

Capitalist Exchange and Exclusive Property

Let's now explore the principles of capitalist economy, particularly as they stem from underlying assumptions about property and possession.[2]

The understanding of property that is bound up with capitalist markets and principles of production tends to identify property with wealth, with material stuff. This is material stuff that might be traded or exchanged for money. This is wealth that one not only enjoys but capital: what is not consumed or used up to meet immediate human needs but used instead for purposes of accumulation, to yield more, to produce profit. To the extent property is not just identified with what one has in one's physical possession but involves a legitimate claim, property tends to mean simply a right to what one already possesses. Property in this sense does not include any right to what one does not have but deserves to, or any right to what is not a possible material possession (for example, the right to develop one's capacities and talents). Nor does it primarily concern rights in things short of possession (right to use what one does not fully own).

Property is, moreover, private in the sense of exclusive ownership;

one has the exclusive or negative right to keep others from the use and enjoyment of what one owns. Only on that condition can property be bought and sold; it makes no sense to put up for sale what both parties to the exchange already have rights to use and enjoy. Property also implies rights to dispose and transfer by explicit contract; only private property, over which one has exclusive rights of possession and use, can be alienated in those ways. Such rights of disposal are unconditional. One has the right to sell or alienate what one owns freely, without social constraint or social obligation. One can do with one's property as one likes (so long as one does not disturb thereby the private property rights of others). In this way the capitalist understanding of property brings with it unlimited rights of individual appropriation.

One's person can be understood to be one's property along these same lines: one has property in one's person. If one has nothing else, one still has one's life and labor power; everyone possesses something —at least oneself and one's capacities for action. This is quintessentially private property in at least the sense of what is exclusively one's own: one's life and labor power are not owed to anybody else; one has the right to exclude others from the use or enjoyment of them; one's person and labor power can be used or enjoyed by others only with one's free consent.

Exclusive property rights to one's person and capacities become the means of justifying all other forms of exclusive property—that is, property in material possessions. If one's labor is one's private or exclusive property, then so too is what comes to one through its use—the wages of that labor and, indirectly, what one purchases with them. One has rights of exclusive possession to what one has worked for.

Property in one's person is private property too in that, at least with reference to one's labor power, it is disposable property—one can sell it and alienate ownership of the products of it. A capitalist market indeed requires persons with this sort of ownership relationship to their own capacity to work, since only on that condition are they free to contract to sell it in exchange for wages. For a certain period of time, one's labor power is not one's own but someone else's; what one makes during that time becomes one's employer's.

It is this ownership relationship with one's labor power that makes contracts between employers and employees seem genuine despite the often huge disparities in material wealth or capital between them. Even if completely destitute, you can enter into a genuinely contractual exchange with your employer, because you still have something valuable to sell. These contracts are also evidently ones upon which one freely enters; even when threatened with starvation, one is rich in labor power and is simply exercising one's right to dispose of it—to sell it off—as one sees fit, in line with one's own best interests. This connection between the idea of self-possession and market legitimacy means that rethinking self-possession threatens to uncover the injustice of market relations in situations of economic inequality—for example, in situations where the institution of private property forces some people to alienate their work and its products for the sake of a decent life.

This logic of property underlying capitalist production and exchange brings with it a certain understanding of social relations. Having property is not viewed as a function of already existing social relations; one does not have the sort of property one does because one is a member of a society organized in a particular way. Instead, social relations are the product of exchanges that only independent persons who already have property engage in freely, to further their own self-interests. Social relations are voluntary or consensual; one enters into them for one's own advantage, to get what one wants or needs. And this freedom to enter into relations of exchange with others is a function of wealth; one must already have something of one's own to exchange. Having property, as suggested before, is what allows one's relations with others to be consensual; if one has property, one is not at the complete mercy of one's fellow human beings but can approach them on something like an equal footing.

The freedom that having property involves is, moreover, primarily understood negatively, almost a-socially, as freedom from others and their potentially unjust seizure or use of what is one's own. One has one's own person and what one has worked for without owing them to anyone else; one does not owe them, in particular, to society, and that is why there are no legitimate social restrictions on what one might do with them. Freedom from others suggests in this way freedom from any rights of needy others to use or enjoy what one has. Exclusive property rights in things and negative freedom mean that this understanding of property is not easily compatible with the idea of rights to well-being on the part of the general populace, or with the idea of a social commitment to furthering the livelihood of all.

Private property, with its exclusive and negative claims against others, is generally understood from a capitalist point of view to be something natural.[3] Often it is taken to be simply a given of societies everywhere. It is just naturally the case that some people have things that other people don't, and that is why they enter into relations of barter and trade: to get from one another the things that they want or need. Everyone is after *things* they want or need, and they enter into exchange relations with *people* just to the extent those other people own those things. Some people have some things; other people have other things. Everything owned is a scarce commodity in that sense, and therefore one must exchange with others to get what one wants. In short, if exclusive ownership of property didn't already exist, there would be no need for barter or trade. These very uncomplicated relationships of barter or trade just gradually expand over time, with the technical help of money, credit institutions, and so on, into full-blown capitalism.

If private property isn't simply a given, the capitalist view is that it is a natural development smoothing the way for exchanges under conditions of scarcity. I don't have what I need in any case. And the institution of private property just helps clear up confusion about how to get it. I now know from whom I can get what I need and can be secure in my possession of it once trade or barter with that person is complete. Everything becomes quite orderly. Or private property is viewed as the only sensible way of preventing conflicts over scarce resources, and therefore it is an almost ineluctable eventuality. There just isn't enough to go around of all the things that people want or need; without the institution of private property there would be chaotic, irresolvable fights going on all the time for possession of everything.

It makes more sense to argue, however, against the usual capitalist self-understanding, that private property—in a capitalist sense of this at least—is not a natural relation that people have with things but a very particular sort of social institution. As such it creates the very conditions of scarcity that lie behind the competitive fights of capitalism. Before the industrialization of Britain, for example, people in the countryside did not lack, in principle, what they needed in order to survive; that happened when the land that they had always used for pasture or hunting was fenced off and turned thereby into private property. Without the means of subsisting on their own, they were willing to be hired for less than what their employers could get out of their labor. This is the gap that makes industrial production profitable, and it sets off the competitive relations between employers and employees that characterize capitalism: employers are always trying to pay their workers less or make do with fewer of them, while workers are always trying to get hired and to raise their wages. Because the value of goods produced is always higher than what workers are paid and because, in general, companies will always try to generate profits at the expense of their workers, the chronic state of capitalism is overproduction: there always tend to be more goods on the market than the workers who are the primary consumers of those goods have the money to buy. The consumer's dollar in this way becomes the scarce resource for which every company has to fight every other to the death. The alternative is loss of profit share, declining profits, and ultimately bankruptcy. At the same time, on the consumer side of things, the impression of scarcity simply increases, for all the frequency of overproduction and market glut. The enormous productive capacities of industry accustom people to needing objects that they could never provide for themselves out of their own resources, such as cars and televisions. I never have the means to make these things for myself; I must always get them from others—from the companies that sell them—using money I make in working for someone else. Human needs are social; what one needs to live is not equivalent to some bare level of subsistence but to the minimum standard of a good life in a particular society at a particular time. In competitive fights with other producers, companies flood the market with all sorts of new products that are subject to the exclusive ownership of private purchase and try, through advertising, for example, to make them the new baseline of a good life. One is never finally able to have, then, all that one needs.

When the understanding of property we have been talking about—property as an exclusive and unconditioned right to use and dispose of what one possesses—combines with the growing dominance of these sorts of competitive markets, the usual result is large inequalities in wealth and all that wealth now buys in opportunities, respect, and responsibilities, without any apparent internal check. Whenever free markets expand to include at least land and resources, exclusive property rights in things possessed foster unequal distributions of wealth to the point where some people have so little that they are significantly disadvantaged relative to others and therefore ripe for exploitation or simple inhuman neglect. Having money or lacking it tends, in short, to become a cumulative condition. If you have money, on the one hand, you can make money—for example, by loaning it to people who don't have as much. The more money that some people have gives them a competitive edge over the money of people with less: they need the money that you have and are willing to pay for it. Markets are geared to those who already have purchasing power; for example, middle-class men worried about erectile dysfunction find an unusually wide range of drug choices on the market for their purchasing pleasure compared to impoverished African women and children dying of AIDS. Their already privileged lives improve, while the others' lives decline even further. Reserves of cash provide a cushion in the face of unexpected problems or economic downturns; a company, for example, doesn't have to put its product on the market when the market is glutted and prices are low, but can wait for better times. If you lack money, on the other hand, every problem likely snowballs into a crisis. You lack the money to get professional help for your child with a disability; you stay at home on an unpredictable basis to attend to her yourself; you lose your job as a result, and have to start over at the lowest rung of the employment ladder if you are ever employed again.[4]

Now that we have some rudimentary understanding of the underlying principles and structures of capitalism and some sense of why they might be worrisome, let's begin to look at the two alternatives to capitalist economy I mentioned earlier, ones that are based on ideas of inalienable property. Do they suggest directions that theology should take in the effort to expand our economic imaginations beyond capitalist presumptions?

Locke, Inalienable Property, and Loan

Let's start with John Locke. His views are sufficiently similar to the understandings of property I've just outlined to be confused with them. But they represent a genuine second logic of property and one that is informed by theological claims in an interesting way: they do not simply tinker with or put the usual capitalist understandings of property rights under constraints but give a fundamentally different understanding of property pride of place.[5]

First of all, if for Locke, very famously, one has a property right to life, liberty, and the pursuit of happiness, property is not easily identifiable with material wealth. Nor is property exclusively associated with a rightful claim to what one already possesses. A significant feature of property for Locke is that it involves an enforceable claim on what one does not own—for example, rights of use to common lands in an economy in which land is only just beginning to become a rightful commodity of mere private possession.[6]

But of much greater significance is the fact that Locke makes inalienable property (property that is not at one's free disposal) and common property (involving positive rights of access on everyone's part to means of subsistence and well-being) the bases for any exclusive rights of possession. For Locke (in keeping with the dominant Christian views of the ancient and medieval church) property rights are inclusive or common at their root: the world and everything in it have been given by God for the good of all, and therefore all have a property right to use the natural resources of the earth so as to maintain their existence and further their well-being. Exclusive property rights are simply the way that this common property right is individuated so as to be actually enjoyed by particular people. In order for anyone to enjoy the common right to land and natural resources to satisfy personal needs and wants, one must make (usually through labor) some part of that land and those resources one's own in an exclusive sense, so that now no one has the right to take them from you or use them without your consent. Individual rights of exclusive appropriation are limited, however, by the same common rights that are their basis: private appropriation is legitimate only to the extent it continues to respect the rightful claims of others to what is necessary for them to exist and flourish.

The exclusiveness of one's property rights is also directly undercut because what one has a right to possess and use has not really been alienated from its true owner, God, the one who made the earth and everything in it and therefore owns them. All private property is on loan or held in tenancy from God, who retains full possession (in some significant sense) and whose purposes—the good of all—must therefore be served if one is to maintain rightful possession. What cannot be made one's full or exclusive property cannot be alienated but only delegated or loaned, through contractual agreements. One cannot, for example, sell what one does not fully own; one can permit others access to it only on the same conditions extended to oneself by the real owner. Therefore what looks like a sale in a capitalist sense of free disposal or transfer of ownership is not really that but the transfer of rights of use with strings attached. Similarly on the political side of things, people delegate, rather than alienate, their property rights to institutions of government, with the understanding that these rights to existence and well-being will be preserved and furthered thereby. People retain these rights in some significant sense and therefore the powers entrusted to government are forfeited upon violation of the people's trust. One could therefore say that the people relate to their government the way God relates to them. In both cases someone is entrusted with something to carry out the intentions of the one handing it over and violation of that trust brings retribution (through the revolt of the people against a corrupt government or God's punishment of people after death).

Locke is a famous proponent of property in one's person and capacities, but this property is fundamentally inalienable in a way it is not under capitalism. Because God owns oneself and one's capacities, one cannot alienate them, or sell them contractually, in any free, no-strings-attached transfer, anymore than one could do that with an apartment one is only renting. Property rights come with God-given conditions—to serve the good of all through the exercise of such rights. One cannot give someone free disposal over oneself (or others) without contravening this sort of obligation to maintain and care for God's property; granting someone rights of free disposal simply means not holding him or her to such an obligation.

Because property in one's person and capacities is inalienable, Locke denies that one can freely contract to be subject to a ruler with absolute power or freely contract to become a slave. Both slave labor and an absolute state require the alienation of property rights that cannot properly be alienated. One cannot transfer to a slave owner or absolute ruler rights of unconditional disposal over one's life and capacities that one does not have oneself.

Capitalism often makes a distinction between one's person and one's capacities when considering such questions of legitimate sale: one can sell one's labor power but not oneself, and if one's labor power is sold without conditions (on, say, the length of time one is going to work), a labor contract blurs illegitimately into sale of one's person. But contrary to Locke's view of one's person and capacities held in tenancy from God, in capitalism one is the full owner of one's person and capacities in a way that makes the alienation of both at least a real possibility. Full liberty over oneself easily suggests, ironically, that, should one feel like it, one can hand it over by contract to someone else. The distinction between one's person and one's capacities is also a hard one to draw for these purposes.[7] Aren't one's capacities to work part of oneself? One can perhaps distinguish between them conceptually or in the abstract, but the two are inseparable in fact, as the situation of working for wages makes clear: an employer may be purchasing only labor power, but that labor power will not do the employer much good unless the worker also shows up! It is therefore easy to suspect that the distinction between one's person and one's labor is simply being employed here ideologically to justify a sharper difference, in principle, between working for wages and slavery than the realities of capitalism would support. Debt-slavery among wage laborers—the de facto enslavement of workers to companies that have extended them credit for purchases at company stores—is, for example, a common practice in many areas of the world.

For Locke, one's person and capacities are also one's own (and not merely God's) in an inalienable way: giving someone else free disposal over them would therefore be to lose one's humanity. Loss of direct self-governance even with respect to one's capacity to act—labor power in the capitalist sense implied by the exchange of labor for wages—would seem then for Locke to slide uncomfortably close to slave labor. One's person certainly cannot be alienated as it is in slavery without the loss of one's humanity, but neither can one's labor power be alienated without a similarly demeaning cost if that means one exchanges for money the bare capacity to act in a way that puts it under the direction of another. One's humanity seems honored in markets for labor only where wages are exchanged for services that remain under the primary direction of the worker and that presuppose the worker's own know-how (as is the case, say, in master/servant relations or pre-capitalist cottage industries).

While Locke's account of property rights goes some way toward undercutting both the primary understanding of property that organizes capitalism and the social relations it justifies, his views are not as radical as they sound, particularly when one considers how Locke puts the various aspects of his account together in explaining its implications for practice. For example, the idea of common right, a right of access to means of subsistence and well-being that one does not presently possess, has potentially radical consequences for any social organization; in none of them do people actually enjoy that right. Locke curtails these radical implications, first of all, through his understanding of what it means for one properly to hold something in tenancy or on loan. The test of proper use of another's property is not positive approximation to the goal—the subsistence and well-being of all—in accordance with which it was handed over originally by God. What the owner intends one to do with it can therefore put only the most minimal constraints on how the property is held or used. God's purposes in creation are merely a negative limit, and, short of that limit, anything goes. All sorts of actual property divisions, so long as they do not involve an absolute and egregious violation of God's plans, are to be deemed legitimate. None of those ways of distributing property is properly considered a candidate for revolutionary overhaul, even were that overhaul to mean that people would come much closer to realizing their common rights than they do now.

Second, work as a requirement for private or exclusive rights undercuts the force of common right. The common right of access to the earth and its resources for one's subsistence and well-being does mean, if one cannot work productively—because of physical incapacity or a growing scarcity in materials on which to work as other people take private possession of natural resources—that one is due charitable assistance. The transfer of unearned exclusive rights to those who do not work is justified in such cases by common right. But these are exceptions to the rule. Ordinarily, the common right becomes one's personal right only to the extent one mixes one's labor with the resources that one has a common right to use. Work, in short, is the usual condition for all private appropriation and possession. One has a right, then, to take from the earth what one needs to survive and live well, but that right is completely emasculated in practice; unless one earns the right to do so through one's own work, none of those resources is properly put to actual use for one's own good. People may not all be enjoying their common right to subsistence and well-being, but there is nothing necessarily wrong with that. Differences in private possession can always be chalked up to differences in the effort that people have put in; some people just work harder than others. The obligation to work is, indeed, written into the conditions of God's original loan, or entrusting, of the earth and its resources to humans. Even though everyone has a right in common to the goods of the earth (and therefore one has a right to charity if one cannot work), one is obligated to work by the original contract between God and human beings: it is only in that way that one serves God's purposes and gains a legitimate right of use to some part of the earth for oneself. The result of all this is Locke's recommendations concerning poor laws: the state's disciplining of poor children to promote a work ethic and the forcing of the able-bodied poor to work.

Third, there is simply some ambiguity here about the import of common right for existing inequalities in the distribution of exclusive property.[8] On the one hand, conditions are placed on the extent of differences in exclusive appropriation: those differences cannot be so great that some people are left to starve; that would violate their common right. On the other hand, common right can be used, in the same way the work requirement can, to justify all sorts of existing differences short of that. Common right suggests, contrary to appearances, that everyone starts out on an equal footing and therefore that the inequalities surfacing now are legitimate: the people who come out on the bottom had the same chance as everyone else; they just didn't use it well. To make the point another way: there is, one could say, an ambiguous import to the way Locke connects common right with exclusive rights of possession.[9] On the one hand, it is not the case for Locke that exclusive property is primary and limited by an entirely different sort of property right—common right—coming into the picture after the fact. Common right is primary, and exclusive property is just the way individuals put that common right into effect. Exclusive rights are therefore naturally or internally constrained by common right. There is no real question then: exclusive property is to be limited by common right as a matter of course. To use a simple analogy: Everybody has the right to sit on the bus. In order to enjoy that right you have to sit down. Once you do, your seat is yours, and nobody else can sit there. But you naturally don't have the right to hog seats where that means depriving others of the same right you have to sit. On the other hand, however, the two are so closely related that common right lacks much critical purchase over exclusive right: exclusive appropriation is the way that individuals realize their common right. Common right is a mere potential; the reality is exclusive possession. There is no such thing, for example, as actual shared possession; Locke's vision of property does not seem to include common lands that would actually be used or appropriated in common.[10] Common right doesn't really mean anything, then, apart from the fact of exclusive forms of appropriation by individuals.

Another major problem for Locke, if he is to provide a genuine alternative to capitalist property rights, is that talk of owning oneself and one's capacities oddly distances oneself from those capacities and even more oddly from one's person, in a way that helps makes sense of their possible status as commodities. Although Locke maintains that they are inalienable at the cost of our humanity, having a proprietary relationship to them clearly suggests that they could be alienated. The individual seems to be separable from, to be in some external or contingent relation to, his or her own person and capacities, and therefore it might well be hard to see how the individual could be seriously diminished or injured through their sale. The individual in that case is no longer identified with the person directing the exercise and development of his or her own capacities; the individual becomes instead the mere repository of labor or talents susceptible to use by others for their own ends. Such a possibility of alienation or grant of free disposal is encouraged, too, by Locke's suggestion that the exercise of one's capacities is not the work of God but one's own work. God owns—and therefore has the right to limit the use of—one's capacities and the materials that one consumes and on which one works, not the actual exercise of those powers through acts of one's own will. That exercise of capacities might seem, then, simply one's own to do with as one sees fit, and not what one holds as a loan subject to conditions set by the real owner, God.

Finally, the reward system behind Locke's understanding of the contract between God and human beings is religiously problematic; it is quite amenable to a two-covenant theology (which Locke himself espoused in *The Reasonableness of Christianity*). The primary covenant is one of works: God hands over something to you on the understanding that you will do what God wants with it. If you do, God will hand over more to you; if you do not, you forfeit your rights and are subject to penalty. The covenant of grace is this covenant of works modified or just differently understood: the same covenant of works is a covenant of grace in that such a covenant exists at all by God's free choice and in that God has made it easy for people to serve God as God requires. What God wants of us is simply rather easy for us to do in light of our God-given capacities (good intentions and right reason). Or if we have a harder time meeting God's requirements, then God (by virtue of what Christ does) mercifully accepts the best one can do in lieu of full performance. In short, the theology underpinning Locke's logic of property and exchange exhibits a rather deflated understanding of God's grace.

Grace, Gift Exchange, and the Freely Given Gift

This absence of a strong sense of grace in Locke's theology might indeed be the key to drawing a sharper contrast with a capitalist logic of property. Ideas about property in one's person, common rights of use and work as a condition for individual appropriation of these rights of access, loan and obligation based on rights that have been entrusted or delegated—all these ideas, I have been suggesting, are too close to the capitalist logic of private property to hold out against it. These ideas, at bottom, go back to a certain understanding of God's relation to the world: God owns the world and everything in it because God made them; we hold all these things from God legitimately for our own good only if we work for them; we are indebted to God for what we so hold, and owe God service; and so on. The same sort of relations that we have with God are then transferred down the line, so to speak, as we delegate, in turn, the property rights we have from God to others, in either private economic contracts or public ones that set up the deal people have with their governments. But what if God is a more gracious God than this? Might not our whole understanding of property and the social relations it underpins shift quite radically along with such a changed theological understanding?

God after all is very rarely thought by Christian theologians to make the world through labor: God speaks, and the world immediately comes to be, without any effort, without materials or tools. God, in short, just does not work, and therefore the effort God expends, the work that God puts into it, cannot be the justification for God's ownership of the world. God's creation of the world in this way establishes no easy basis for human proprietary relationships based on work, distributions of property that conform to effort.[11]

Moreover, what if God does not offer this world to us on any kind of contract suggesting private property? What if the picture is not one in which God has exclusive ownership of the goods of life until we exchange what we have and what God wants from us for them—our lives of service, our worship, our very hearts and minds? What if God does not even loan the world to us on conditions set by God's continued ownership of it, like some big landlord in the sky? What if God simply gives us what we need in an utterly gracious way? And expects us to organize our lives with one another accordingly? The categories of gift and grace, then, might contrast sharply with both Locke's and a capitalist logic of property, and suggest the possibility of an interesting new one.

As a first step in developing such an economy of grace or gift, it might make sense to look at a theologian who has a much more robust account of grace, despite employing many of the same notions of tenancy, loan, and stewardship as Locke does when discussing human responsibility before God. For example, in the theology of John Calvin—a Protestant reformer who emphasized the sovereignty of God's grace in a way he thought lacking in much previous theology—the dominant motif, one might argue, is the supreme graciousness of God's fatherly beneficence.[12] From the ever overflowing fountain of God's own goodness made accessible in Christ, this fatherly God bestows all the goods of life, freely and liberally, upon cherished children, who may be running wild in their sin, but for whose sake this father continues to do everything he can. The other Christian vocabulary of loan, tenancy, and so on, with quite ancient roots—and quite common then before and after Locke—is set within this dominant motif of gracious beneficence or placed in some tension alongside it.

On the one hand, there is only a single covenant of grace for Calvin that involves the free gift of mercy to the undeserving. God is not a harsh taskmaster paying wages to servants but a doting parent of wayward children lovingly chastised and rewarded despite their faults simply because they are God's own, the heirs to the parent's fortune and in whom God wishes only to delight.[13] All that we do is by God's grace, and therefore the very notion of merit is destroyed.[14] We receive a reward not because our works earn it but because God out of kindness has simply set that value on what we do.[15] We are to keep the law as an act of honor, reverence, and gratitude, not as any simple obligation externally imposed by divine demand.

On the other hand, however, God does seem to be setting us a task, to be greeted by either rewards or penalties. We should use God's gifts for the purpose for which he gave them to us.[16] They have been entrusted to our use as stewards, and we must one day render an account of them; a reckoning will one day be made of our use of them.[17] God's gifts are held by us like "the usufruct of a field by another's liberality," and therefore when we do what the owner of the title of the property requires of us, we "have only carried out services owed."[18] We do not need to pay the debt of perfect performance of God's law or the penalty for failure to so perform, but someone still has to—Christ.[19] Looking to that perfect payment, God overlooks our own failure to provide what is due and, upon that forgiveness, gives us the benefits that are the reward of it, the benefits that are properly owed to someone perfectly obedient.[20]

One can put together these two sides of Calvin's theology so that they involve a fundamental disruption of the logic of debt and loan, but it is very hard to avoid entirely the suggestion here that grace and liberality are simply being made to fit a context of legal requirement. Legal requirement remains, one can just as easily argue, the dominant paradigm even while it is being contested. Combining the language of grace with the language of tenancy and loan in the way Calvin does seems as prone to subvert the language of gift as to subvert the language of loan and debt.

Could one, instead, make the idea of grace the incontrovertible and perhaps exclusive organizing principle of a theological economy? Eschewing even ownership in the form of a loan, could one develop what it means to hold oneself and the whole of the world as gifts of God and then ask about the character that legitimate social exchanges might take on that basis?

Theologians who have suggested something like this—Stephen Webb, John Milbank, Catherine Pickstock, and to a lesser extent M. Douglas Meeks—have been drawn to models of noncommodity gift exchange in non-Western locales not yet fully subject to market conditions.[21] In such economies of exchange, possessions seem always shared in a fluid circuit, ever returning to their initiating source and flowing out again to meet needs in what looks irresistibly to these theologians like some sort of this-worldly imitation of (or participation in) the mutual love among trinitarian persons. But to what extent are such noncommodity gift exchanges really very different from the logics of property we have previously discussed?

It is common, indeed, simply to contrast these non-Western gift exchanges in, say, beads or shells across the South Sea Islands with commodity exchanges in capitalist markets. Thus, "commodity exchange is an exchange of alienable things between transactors who are in a state of reciprocal independence. . . . Non-commodity (gift) exchange is an exchange of inalienable things between transactors who are in a state of reciprocal dependence."[22] Unlike commodity exchange between strangers, gift exchange occurs between familiars; it presupposes or brings about close relations of interdependence—relations of trust or agonistic mutual comparison. The focus is not so much on goods exchanged and what they represent for one's individual well-being as on the relationships between people that are brought about by such exchanges. Objects themselves, then, have a social meaning more than a directly material one; possession is important for what it indicates about one's social standing vis-à-vis one's fellow transactors. It is not actual possession, moreover, that increases that status. One's social standing goes up the more one gives away to others rather than the more one receives from them. Receiving from others tends to put one in a one-down position, in a position of debt to the giver, from which one is eager to extricate oneself by giving away what one has received. The goal of exchange for the individual is to maximize what one puts out—the more one gives, the more one benefits through the accrual of prestige—in contrast to commodity exchanges, where the goal is to accumulate or take in as much as one can for oneself.

One does not enter these exchanges as an individual for one's own independent reasons, but as a participant in a society that requires these sorts of exchanges from its members. The exchanges are just one of society's fundamental organizing principles. Unlike market exchange in the West, in non-Western gift exchange one is therefore not free to enter into or refuse exchange. Instead, gift giving is sustained through a system of social obligations: everyone must give when able, accept gifts offered, and give in return.

Social relations do not end when a return is made, as they do in relations between buyers and sellers. Return "payment" only solidifies the relationship and provides a basis for its continuation. Making a return as one is obligated to—even returning more than one has been given as a sort of interest for benefits accrued through possession and use—does not cancel debt but continues it. It merely puts a similar obligation back on the other party; it merely increases or adds to the nexus of obligation by making the original giver indebted as well. In this way gift relations are self-sustaining, without the periodic or episodic and sequential character of commodity exchanges, in which a completed exchange of money for goods or services breaks off relations with one person to make way for exchange with someone else.

Unlike commodity exchange, which gives the impression that objects are being brought into relation via the people who own them, here persons are brought into relation by the objects they exchange. The person from whom you get the object therefore becomes as important as the object itself; it matters, for example, whether you received this from a person of high or low status. Objects, for the same reason, are not fungible the way they are in commodity transactions. When I put down my money for a television set, I don't care which television of the same make and model, in the same pristine factory-fresh condition, is brought out from the shop's storage room for me. In noncommodity gift exchange, one object cannot be replaced with another, no matter how similar they might be to one another, if they do not come to you from the hands of the same people or at least people of a similar social status. There is, indeed, no sharp distinction here between objects and persons of exchange, between objects and their owners, as in commodity exchange. Instead, objects themselves are personalized in ways that suggest they cannot be alienated from their givers. The fact that objects personify their givers is one reason why they obligate return to their original owners.

Finally, unlike commodity contract, return, while obligatory, should never be immediate but always delayed. In the delay the gift's ability to generate debt is increased by being passed on to others so as to establish a longer string or stream of debt. Return giving should not be transparent in the search for equivalency (say, by return of the very same thing). Nor should the price of the gift (and the interest it brings) be calculated and thereby the character of a fair return established by explicit agreement. Because there is no explicit contract about the terms, gift exchanges are open to a greater degree of creativity and skill than one typically finds in the execution of a commodity contract. One might not be free to enter or exit the gift circuit, but in the midst of it one has more freedom to maneuver than commodity contracts generally allow.

These contrasts with commodity exchange are, however, easily overblown.[23] Gift exchange has some clear analogies with capitalist exchange. In both, the use-value of objects, their capacity to meet human needs, is not primarily at issue. At stake in gift exchange is one's social standing and social prestige. One's material needs are not directly met through these exchanges but by the alternative means of barter, cultivation of common or private property, or simple seizure. Often, indeed, the objects exchanged, while considered highly valuable, are useless—beads, shells. They are not the sort of objects that meet material needs and are forbidden from being exchanged for material goods. The point of capitalist exchange, in a similar fashion, is not primarily to consume what one purchases, but to make money off it—by manufacturing other goods with it or by selling it for more than one paid. And what is often most valuable about what one has or about the money one makes is not the way it enables one to satisfy one's needs in high style, but the simple prestige value of capitalist profit and the objects it enables one to buy. The more money one is able to make through capitalist forms of exchange, the higher one's social standing. Ideally, one has accumulated more than one could ever use in a lifetime; the equivalent of the GNP (Gross National Product) of all of Africa, for example, would be nice and surely ensure one's invitations to the best parties! It is not so much the character of an expensive car's ride that makes its owner the envy of the neighbors, but what it cost; using one's money to purchase useless objects such as works of art has a high prestige value something like gift-exchange shells; and so on.

Rather than bring about the meeting of needs, the primary effect of both is to organize social relations in a distinctive way—for example, in the impersonal fashion of capitalist exchange or the more person-specific mode of gift exchange. Exchange in both cases produces, moreover, a kind of increase or profit—that is the defining feature of capital, in the one case, and of giving across multiple recipients, in the other. Gifts in fact circulate similarly to the way money does when it becomes capital. Like the gift, money is not spent once and for all but only with the intention of getting it back through its passage from one hand to another; the money that is used to purchase things in capitalist exchange is always eventually turned back into money in a kind of ever-renewed spiral. Capitalist exchanges are also commonly subject to risks and delays that make strict calculation of returns impossible.[24] A contract for the sale of property might be quite rigid in its terms, but manufacturing for the consumer market always involves uncertainties: one throws one's product onto the market without any guarantees that anyone will buy it for more than what it cost to produce.

Capitalist markets are based on competition, but gift exchanges too have a competitive tendency. The giving of gifts establishes relations of superiority and subordination: the giver has status and is due a return gift or, short of that, return service. "Between chiefs and their vassals, between vassals and their tenants, through such gifts a hierarchy is established. To give is to show one's superiority, to be more, to be higher in rank. . . .To accept without giving in return, or without giving more back, is to become client and servant, to become small, to fall lower."[25] While gifts and return gifts can be balanced, the flexible, incalculable character of exchange, along with the tendency of increase through further giving, makes such balance very hard to achieve and rarely very clear. Competition among gift givers is therefore not unusual: often an initial gift is more than matched by a return gift, setting off a chain reaction, whereby each struggles to maintain the upper hand in relations of indebtedness.

One can argue, further, that gift exchanges simply become commodity contracts when the parties to them become strangers or, even more precisely, simply become loans when directed to outsiders.[26] Gift exchanges are implicitly contractual by virtue of the conditions placed on exchange: you do not establish a relationship with someone by giving to them unless they can do something for you—unless they can be relied on later to help you harvest your crops, or unless they have the sort of social prestige that will prove your greatness when you give more to them than they give to you. Gift exchanges are also, at bottom, implicitly contractual because of the obligations they enforce on all sides.[27] This contractual aspect—that is, the fact that one must make a return gift, that giving a gift requires a return—must be occluded by the participants: one cannot point it out without the loss of the gift character of the exchange. The contract is not spelled out but remains vague, and seems to depend on trust among intimates or, less charitably, on their awareness that they simply cannot do without each other and have no other choice. When such trust is lost or people have greater independence from one another, the terms of the contract have to be made explicit and definite, immediate returns become preferable (since one cannot be certain that those indebted to you are trustworthy), and external reinforcement of obligation becomes necessary—for example, through codified law and the police. Focus shifts thereby to the objects—what they are worth—and away from the subjects who are parties to the exchange. And struggles for status do too.

To the extent the last major difference between the two remains—objects of exchange are inalienable from their givers—this simply means that gift exchanges turn into explicit loans.[28] Requirement of return to the giver, the fact that a gift is never finally alienated from its giver, suggests that gifts are a kind of common property or loan never fully possessed by the recipient. Locke's economy is therefore something very much like a gift economy—just one with explicit conditions, more calculation, and special institutions of enforcement (and monetary payment for rights of use, or rent). They both envision a world that runs on debt and credit, in which primary obligations derive from the delegation, or holding in trust, of inalienable property.

If Locke's economy of inalienable property has problems, it is unclear why one should expect anything better from noncommodity gift economies. Indeed, far worse than anything we saw in Locke, all that the features distinguishing a gift economy from an explicit debt economy like Locke's produce is a world of infinite debt. Debts can never be completely paid off; they simply multiply without end. For similar reasons, once it starts up, competition for prestige, disconnected from the meeting of needs, presses on to absurd lengths; nothing curbs it. The result is potlatch: destruction of vast quantities of goods as proof of the giver's superiority. The relations between superiors and subordinates that giving establishes—the fact that getting a gift is never an entirely good thing, especially if you are poor or young or both and therefore without much to give back—promotes the ideal of an unpayable debt, one that would spell ineradicable domination. If God is such a giver, God is just the biggest of "big men."

Much as we saw with Locke, the lack of distinction between persons and things—holding one's person not in this case as inalienable property but in the form of a gift to be given to others—means here that some people, most often women, are very much treated as things, simple objects of exchange. Gifts become separable from the giver (much as we saw for Locke person and capacities can become separable from oneself as one's property); some people then become the gifts that other people give and receive. Self-giving that one directs oneself is replaced by forms of exchange that could easily devolve into simple exploitation.[29]

Ironically confirming my point about the limited resources of gift-exchange economies for an economy of grace, such exchanges have much more in common with loans or commodity contracts than they do with philanthropic or charitable giving.[30] It is giving to the needy that gift exchange most differs from. Charitable giving meets the needs of the recipient. The point is not to keep the gift circulating but to allow it to settle with the one who needs it; the one who receives it is to consume it, use it up. At least in the philanthropic or charitable giving we are familiar with in the United States, donor and recipient are commonly strangers, and giving does not establish ongoing relations between them. The point of the giving is not to keep the relationship up. To the contrary, charitable giving often justifies the donor's not having anything further to do with the recipient. The giving of gifts now means that the recipient can be excluded in good conscience from all the usual social or exchange relations that make up the donor's life. The fact of charitable giving might help to legitimate, for example, the fact that one is not empowering the recipient for the sort of participation in capitalist exchange that might make him or her less needy. Unlike gift exchange, in which circulation seems almost to become an end in itself, the important thing about charitable giving is the gift and the benefits it brings to others, not the act of giving and receiving or the sort of relationship it sets up. A gift that does not benefit others is simply not a gift to charity, while gift exchange is perfectly compatible with gifts whose only purpose is to belittle or cut their recipients down to size. Revenge killings, honor killings, might even make a good gift exchange; the exchange of acts of revenge might perfectly well exhibit the usual characteristics of gift exchange—for example, the way returns work only to sustain further exchanges, the never completed character of gift exchange.[31] In keeping with this lack of attention to relationship, charitable gifts are typically alienated from their givers; they do not remain in any sense the giver's possession, and therefore in being received do not attach one to the giver. And they are handed over in no-strings-attached transfers; what was once yours is now someone else's, and the recipient generally can do with it what he or she likes. No return is obligated; indeed, charitable gifts are often made anonymously in ways that prevent returns to the giver. At most one merely expects the recipient's gratitude, a "thank you" that at its chilliest simply acknowledges the donor's having already done more than enough and that therefore represents the recipient's agreement not to subject the donor to further pleas for aid.

We can conclude, then, from this exploration of gift-exchange economies that it does not make sense to model an economy of grace on them. Their underlying principles do not represent much of an alternative to either capitalist exchange or loan-based economies like the one Locke advocated. Nor are they very attractive—to say the least—on their own terms. The sense of gift that organizes our economy of grace should be fundamentally different from the sense of gift in gift-exchange economies. The odd spin or response that a theology formed with reference to them should give to the principles of gift-exchange is rejection.

The discussion so far is helpful, nonetheless. To develop an economy of grace, we need to move beyond, it now seems, both contracts that presuppose private property and conditional loans or grants associated with inalienable forms of possession. The sense of gift or grace that organizes our reading of the Christian story should fundamentally undercut principles of exchange of all those sorts. Notions of debt, contractual obligation, loan, even stewardship, should be written out of the Christian story about God's relations to the world and our relations with God and one another, in light of an understanding of grace that is fundamentally incompatible with them.

But what sense of grace is that? Presumably, it is closer to what we ordinarily mean by gift than to the sense of gift in gift-exchange economies. In this ordinary sense, giving is defined directly over and against loan and sale in a very explicit way. We ordinarily think of a gift as what is not being loaned or sold to one. Indeed, the meaning of giving is proved, almost refined, by efforts to exclude from it all aspects of loan and sale. No reciprocity or exchange is at all necessary for it. A gift is offered freely and not as any kind of tit-for-tat, certainly not as a return for services rendered. It comes with no strings attached of an obligatory kind, as loans do; you are free to respond as you like and only if you feel like it. A gift is offered for nothing, without compensation, apart from any consideration of a return being made for it. Giving is completely disinterested, without self-concern, solely for the well-being or pleasure of others.

Of course we are familiar with the way gifts in our society assume many of the characteristics of gifts in noncommodity gift economies.[32] Gifts commonly do form a circuit of reciprocal exchange. Gifts are exchanged, for example, among family members at Christmas or among friends when their birthdays roll around. Often the result is that you end up pretty much with what you started with: the money you put out for that tie for Dad on Father's Day comes right back to you in a shirt for your birthday. One-upping one's siblings in the gift department on Christmas morning can set up a struggle with them for parental favor. We are familiar with the way giving becomes de rigueur: a brother must give his little sister a birthday present whether he wants to or not. We recognize, moreover, the way gifts are often used to control others: the money your father is giving you for college tuition ends up being a way of getting you to break off a love affair he disapproves of. We know, too, how inheriting one's parents' money is often a matter of whether one has been the sort of son or daughter they wanted.

But the difference here is that none of this is required any longer for giving. Giving still has a social sense in the absence of all that. You are still making a present of something, in the usual sense of that, when it stands no chance of being reciprocated and when any advantage to you is completely out of the question. Moreover, the very norm for giving becomes the absence of those things; a gift is more truly, more genuinely a gift the less those typical features of gift-exchange economies make an appearance. Something is not really a gift, then, if it simply reflects the duties of one's social role—sons are just expected to do that sort of thing. A real gift has to have the spontaneous expression of good will behind it, over and above the call of duty. You know something is really a gift only when it is not being used to put pressure on you, when the gift is given simply for your benefit and is not serving any ulterior motive. And so on.

This is a sense of giving that forms historically only when the many functions—particularly the economic ones—served by giving in gift-exchange economies separate off into their own distinct arenas of life.[33] The people with whom you exchange gifts are no longer necessarily the same people upon whom you depend for your economic well-being or the people with reference to whom one's social standing is determined. Status concerns or worries about survival need no longer infiltrate, then, the giving of gifts. Status rivalry can be shifted into some other arena of life: the way one gives or gets gifts is not what primarily establishes one's social rank; the clothes you wear or the car you drive or the job you hold can do that. Similarly, rather than keep them on a kind of retainer (because of their status as your gift-exchange partners), you can simply pay the people you need to work for you. You don't need that neighbor, whose friendly relations you cemented with a dinner and the loan of your lawn mower, to jump-start your car when its battery is dead; you call your local automobile club.

The giving of gifts in this way is purified of other motives—motives that seem to have complicated the gift-exchange economies of earlier centuries in the West, motives that are now set off in opposition to those of gift giving so as to organize, for example, discrete areas of distinctly commercial exchange. "*Gift-exchange*—in which persons and things, interest and disinterest are merged—has been fractured, leaving gifts *opposed* to exchange, persons *opposed* to things and interest to disinterest."[34] The idea of purely disinterested gifts therefore arises at the same time as the idea of purely interested exchanges, and they come to sit side by side as opposites: "these gifts are defined as what market relations are not—altruistic, moral and loaded with emotion."[35] Pure giving—like pure love or pure art for art's sake—simply has nothing to do with the economic, now that the economic has nothing to do with it.

Many theologians find these ideas of purified giving very resonant, as they stand, with God's grace. At most, the theologian just needs to follow through on this effort of purification, purifying giving of economic concerns completely: then you have the sort of giving that God exhibits.[36] But this simply won't do for an economy of grace. First of all, the more giving is purified, the less it appears to be a principle for the organization of society generally, or the basis for an alternative economy, more specifically. Pure giving retreats into the private sphere of purely personal relations; you give purely only to those you love or feel affection for—your family or friends or people whom you would like to make your family and friends. Because it is anti-economic, giving cannot set up relations between employers and employees or, for that matter, establish the character of the bond that citizens feel for their country. Gifts simply become the "symbolic media for managing the emotional aspects of relationships," in very small, face-to-face social worlds, isolated from larger, more impersonal social scenes.[37]

That wider world is thereby left to its own devices, without any challenge being offered to it from principles of pure giving. Personal relations of pure giving, indeed, presuppose and build on the very social and economic spheres they oppose. Rather than challenging private property, one simply takes the money one earns under capitalist forms of exchange and buys a gift for one's beloved with it. Gifts may symbolize one's feelings for someone, but they remain private property and are alienated the way private property is. If you don't fully own something, it is not yours to give away. Once you hand over possession to someone else, you ordinarily cannot ask for the gift back, and recipients have the right to do with gifts as they please—return them to the store for cash, hide them away in a closet—even if the donor's feelings might be hurt were they to know. The voluntary character that defines free markets—individuals have the freedom to choose where and when to apply for work—is carried over to personal gift relations:

you freely choose your gift partners when gift giving is pure. Most significant, personal relations with others simply cannot be purified of economic concerns unless one enjoys a certain economic status.[38] If you don't have the money to buy the services you need, you are going to have to depend on friends and neighbors in relations that gifts or favors back and forth help to solidify. Not a lot of pure giving in the ghetto, then; the underground economy there is often just one big gift-exchange economy. Rather than disputing the validity of capitalist exchange, disinterested giving for the sake of others often simply legitimates the wealth amassed thereby. Bill Gates is such a generous man; his enormous accumulation of capital cannot be all that bad. Sporadic, individual acts of a purely charitable nature mean the system does not need fixing.

Pure giving could in principle extend to everyone and thereby become the principle for social relations generally. Unlike giving with mixed motives, in which one's economic well-being and social standing are also at stake, nothing stops purified giving from being extended indiscriminately—to those who could harm or help you, to those with no bearing on your fortunes, to those of high status or low, and so forth. If a gift is pure, anyone could be chosen to be its recipient. Anyone could be, but few people ever are: pure gifts are rare, exceptional events, proffered typically to just that special someone.

The purer giving is, the more it retreats, indeed, from social relations generally, to the interior of one's emotional life. Pure gifts are a manifestation of pure feeling; they are simply a way of displaying how one feels about someone, how much one loves them. A kind of solipsistic focus on one's interior life in this way restricts the relevance of pure giving for economic questions. It just does not matter, for example, whether one's gifts actually benefit the one to whom they are given: it is the thought that counts.

The purity of the gift is determined by the purity of one's interior dispositions, by the purity of one's inner motive, one's complete lack of self-interest in giving. Again, the effect of this focus on interiority is to limit the economic relevance of giving. It is possible, although the gift happens to cost you nothing, that you would give even at your own expense, at great cost to yourself. It is also possible for one's motive to remain pure despite the possible or actual benefits that might accrue to one in giving to others. The fact that you are going to get a benefit—a return present, someone's kisses—does not necessarily mean, for example, that you are giving to others for that reason. Your gift might remain simply the pure expression of your own feelings and wish to do your beloved a good turn. Presumably, you would make your gift even were a return like that to be unlikely; your giving would be unaffected either way. But since motive is everything, one should not take any chances here.[39] Your lack of self-concern is proved only when you are deprived of what you give, when giving comes at your own expense, when giving comes at a complete loss to yourself. Purity of motive is secured and assured only when there is no possibility of a return of any sort—not even gratitude, not even self-congratulation concerning one's generosity. If the gift were to be received, the recipients might be tempted to make a return. It is best, then, that they don't receive it—best if they refuse to accept it. If they do receive it, it would be great if they did not recognize it as a gift; the fact of giving should therefore be hidden. If they do manage to recognize it as a gift, they must not know from whom they got it. Complete anonymity in giving is a must; the recipients might like to give something back, but they won't know where to direct it. In case they find out who gave it to them, it would be a good idea if the gift is not appreciated; the recipients should not like their presents—no temptation to make a return, then! To prevent one's congratulating oneself on the attempt, it would be preferable indeed if one completely misjudged the recipients' likes and dislikes and they reacted to one's gifts with horror and disdain. One shouldn't even be aware of one's giving, lest that tempt one to pat oneself on the back. And so on, to produce a completely anti-economic understanding of gift, with absolutely no potential to form an alternative economy comparable to the one presently in place. In the best-case scenario you sacrifice your own interests and those of others on the altar of a pure motive. No one else benefits, and you don't either. Hardly a promising economic vision of social well-being.

Giving that is not conditioned by considerations of exchange does, nevertheless, form the bedrock of the economy of grace as I understand it. This sense of unconditioned giving does not, however, allow concerns over purity of motive to get in the way of the effort to benefit others. Nor are worries about whether giving is genuinely disinterested permitted to rule out giving that is in any way beneficial to oneself. The priority is extending benefits. That is what unconditioned giving is all about, after all: an extension of benefits beyond the usual conditions placed on them in loans and sales. You are the proper recipient of benefits whether or not you can pay for them or have done the giver a good turn, even if you've misused them, and so forth. Self-preoccupied worries about purity of motive are allowed to obstruct this goal of benefit only when one's priorities are misplaced.

Whether one's motives are perfectly disinterested is not anything that one should be worried about in any case. In order to distinguish unconditioned giving from any hint of loan or sale, I will suggest, indeed, that giving in an economy of grace is not just unconditioned by what we would ordinarily consider payments or returns for service, but simply unconditional—without any conditions at all. If there are no conditions on giving, one is working toward an absolutely inclusive extension of benefit by giving. There is simply no reason to think this inclusive extension of benefits would exclude oneself, and there is therefore no reason to think any speck of self-concern vitiates the effort. Disinterest is no longer the norm for giving.

Unconditional giving, as I understand it, is just not defined by motive or feeling of any kind; it takes on instead a structural sense. The fact that giving is unconditioned by considerations of exchange—that giving is neither itself a payment nor something requiring payment—is proved, not by the character of the interior dispositions of the giver, but by the structural character of the social relations that such giving should produce. So long as others are benefited whether or not they have done anything to deserve those benefits, and so long as returns are not required of the beneficiaries as a condition of their receipt, the motive behind the giving—for example, how pure the motive was—is really of no additional concern. It doesn't matter what you felt about them, whether you had an uncompromised love for them or whether your giving lacked all self-interest.

Unconditional giving is not a matter of feeling or interior disposition but a social matter, an economic matter, a question of the way benefits are distributed to form social relations. And because it is not fundamentally an expression of emotion, the social relations it forms need not be restricted to those of close friends or kin, limited to exclusive tight-knit groups that approximate families ("brotherhoods"), or relegated to private worlds. Unconditional giving can spread out to become a broad social force, a fundamental principle for the organization of society generally.

Unconditional Giving

If human relations are structured in a way that reflects the character of God's own giving, they should be marked by unconditional giving—that is, giving that is not obligated by the prior performance of the recipients and that is not conditional upon a return being made by them. This principle marks all these relations off from *do ut des* giving, or "I give so that you will give," the alternative principle of conditional giving that covers barter, commodity exchange, and debtor–creditor relations of all sorts.

God does not give gifts to us because of what we have done to deserve them. They are not payments for services rendered. They are not owed by the fulfillment of some prior condition. This is shown, first of all, by God's gift of creation, by the way God gives in creating the world and everything in it. God's creating of the world cannot be a response to anything creatures have done, since God makes a total gift here; God brings into existence the whole of what is from the bottom up, without its existing in any respect before God acts to create it. Prior to God's creating the world, there is nothing, then, to the world to obligate God's creating of it. This same character of giving is evident, second, in the way God sets up covenant relations with Israel. God makes a partnership with Israel unilaterally, from sheer free beneficence and not because of this particular people's special merits.[40] One sees this form of giving, finally, in the way the gifts of salvation are offered to human beings in Christ. They seem to be given to us simply because of our need, our sufferings and incapacities, not because of our righteousness and bountiful living in communities where justice and peace reign, not because of our good use of gifts already given. Christ is the way God comes, not to the righteous and the already blessed, who fully expect their privileges of moral standing and good fortune to bring with them all the further goods of life, but to sinners in the midst of their sin, to the poor crushed by burdens of pain and injustice, to all who seem to be owed nothing.

God's giving is not conditional upon a proper return being made by us for it. God continues to give for our benefit whatever our response might be. And this is a good thing, too, since mired in sin as we are, no one but the God-man Christ ever makes a proper return to God. God simply never stops giving even when we fail to make an entirely proper return. God maintains a gift-giving relation with us, however fragile the exhibition of those gifts in our lives or corrupt our performance in response to their being given. As God's creatures, a continuing relationship with God is the condition of our continuing to live, move, and breathe; if we continue to have the time and space of this created existence, despite our failings, God must be maintaining this gift-giving relationship with us from God's side.

God still gives and is willing to give more; that seems to be God's only reaction to failed response. The human race falls, but God establishes a covenant with Israel—a gift far greater than the goods of mere creation—and maintains a steadfast faithfulness to it, keeps the covenant in force from God's side, even when the human partners to it do not always manage to live up to it. In Christ God gives the greatest gift of God's own life even to the worst sinners, indeed especially to them, just to ease their burden of sin. And when the gifts of salvation fail to make their mark on Christians, God has only other gifts to offer: at the communion rail we can come to feed on Christ when we falter.

God does not stop giving to us because we have misused and squandered the gifts that God has given us. God's gifts are not on loan to us on the condition that we use them rightly, failures in attentive stewardship thereby bringing their forfeiture. It may seem to us as if God takes away gifts in response to our sin. But it is our sin itself that interrupts the reception and distribution of God's gifts, bringing suffering and death in its train. The loss of what we might have enjoyed is not God's punishment of us, but the natural consequence of our turning away from and refusing what God is offering us for our good. God's gifts continue to stream forth to us in the way they always have; we are simply failing to avail ourselves of them, to our own destruction and harm.

If God does not punish in response to sin, it cannot be the case that Christ on the cross is being punished by God in our stead, suffering the loss of what we rightfully should lose because of the way we have misused God's gifts. Nor is Christ, by some supreme act of obedience on the cross, returning us to God's favor by meeting, for once, the conditions for that favor that we were never willing or able to fulfill.[41] There just aren't any such conditions for God's favor. The cross simply doesn't save us from our debts to God by paying them. If anything, the cross saves us from the consequences of a debt economy in conflict with God's own economy of grace by canceling it. We are ransomed on the cross from the suffering and oppression in which a debt economy has thrown us; snatched out of a world of deprivation and injustice from which we suffer because of our poverty, our inability to pay what others demand of us; and returned to God's kingdom of unconditional giving. In Christ we see the manner of divine action that the Jubilee traditions of the Hebrew Bible aimed to reflect: debts forgiven rather than paid, debtors freed from the enslavement that comes from inability to pay, and the return of goods forfeited because of unpaid debts, received back without proper restitution from the creditors who had seized possession of them.[42]

But can we really still say that God's giving is unconditional when we fail in fact to receive and make a proper response to it? Isn't God's giving dependent on the existence of someone willing to receive and respond appropriately to it? In order to be giving, I have suggested, God's giving does not require any of that. God's act of giving is not conditional upon our reception or proper response in that God's giving still streams forth in the same fulsome way even when it meets the brick wall of our sin. This sort of independence from reception and response does not, however, imply that reception and response are irrelevant to God's giving. This independence doesn't hold because whether we receive God's gifts and make use of them for our benefit are beside the point where God's giving is concerned. The reason for it is not, as with a pure gift, that the act of giving is an end in itself and fundamentally defined by the giver's interior state. The whole point of God's giving is to benefit us. A giving essentially concerned in this way with its reception would indeed suggest, at first glance, a giving impaired to some degree should we refuse or misuse it. But additional considerations in God's case block this suggestion of giving conditioned by the character of its effects. First of all, some of God's gifts simply cannot fail to be received; our efforts to refuse always come too late. Our very life, for instance, is the gift of God; we have to have received it to our benefit before we can come to reject it. For God to give here is simply equivalent to our reception and display of the gift's goodness in our lives, in much the way the Father's giving to the Son and Spirit immediately collapses into their proper reception and response—of giving back to the Father.

But this kind of inevitability of reception and benefit doesn't hold for most of God's gifts of creation and covenant: God doesn't make me a saint, and I don't enjoy the benefits of that life, unless and until I begin to act like one. Or perhaps more precisely, inevitable reception of the goods of God's creation is one thing; inevitable proper response to them is another thing entirely—especially for everyone who isn't a saint! Apart from any acts of reception and before I make anything of them, I may simply find myself, from birth, with a host of God-given good capacities, but that doesn't mean I act on them for the good of myself and others. To the contrary, I start to squander any number of them right away, and they are effectively lost to me. I no longer have it in me to do what is good and right.

There is a sort of remedy for this in Christ. Whether we have accepted them or not and however we may respond to them, the goods of God's own life are already and forever ours in Christ by virtue of the fact that God has become one with our humanity there. Christ indeed is the way God has of giving to us—of changing the character of our fundamental property, so to speak, that makes us what we are—whatever we might do, despite ourselves, even while we remain sinners. Even though we reject them, even though we misuse those we accept, the gifts of God are and remain ours in Christ by virtue of what God has already done irrevocably for us—made our humanity suffering under the burden of sin one with God's Word. We have received in a certain sense, then, the gifts of God in Christ before we make anything of them; they are ours before they "take," before we come to accept them and before they act to alter the way we live. And whatever we make of them, they remain. These gifts are ours, a part of us in an inextricable fashion, even when we persistently refuse them or put them to ill use.

Finally, the unconditionality of God's giving is saved despite all our failures of reception and response because anything that might look like a condition for the reception and good use of God's gifts is really itself the gift of God. There is nothing good about us that is not also the gift of God, and this includes the acts by which we receive those gifts and put them to good use. The law and the real ability to act on it are made God's gifts to Israel along with the gift of God as its covenant partner. In and through Christ, God supplies from out of God's own stores to those whose lives are otherwise absent them the worshipful and holy forms of life that are characteristic of God's people. It is, moreover, what is already ours in Christ that enables us to receive Christ with faith and to act in ways our sin would otherwise forbid. Rather than being a condition for the reception of Christ—something that conditions the supposedly unconditional giving of God—faith is therefore just a further consequence, a further gift, of the gift of Christ to us.

To a certain extent it just does not make sense to talk of our making a return to God. One cannot pay God back for what God has given, because God already has all that one might want to give back. The triune God already has, and in greater abundance, with a fullness unimaginable, all that we would like to present to God in exchange for what we have received. God has no need, and therefore God is not giving to us in order to remedy it. There is no lack in God, and therefore God in creating the world is not trying to fill it. The point of God's giving is the world's benefit, and not God's. God is trying to communicate the goodness of God's own life outward to what is not God; picture the overflow of something overly full or the effulgent radiance of something supremely bright. Even in the Trinity, where the Father's giving always finds a return, always finds its match in the giving of the other two persons back to the Father, this is a giving without need and in that sense without the requirement of return. Although the Father is not the Father without these relations of giving among Father, Son, and Spirit, one would not say that the Father is missing anything in and of himself and therefore in need of the return they make: the fullness of the Godhead dwells in the Father; the Father already has everything that the Son and Spirit are returning.

One also cannot make an adequate return for God's giving. Not in the sense that we can never pay enough or that there always remains more to pay, an infinite debt to bear, but in the sense that the very idea of an adequate return loses its meaning here. It is out of the question, first of all, for us to give back to God in the way God has given to us, since we simply lack God's capacities: God creates what God gives from the bottom up, and creatures are at least partly defined simply by their inability to do that. Expecting us to make a return in kind would, then, be asking us to be what God never intended us to be. In the second place, we have nothing that is simply our own to give back to God in payment, since all that we have has been given by God. There is nothing more to us; we have nothing more to give out of our own stores than what we have received. The whole of creatures is God's gift in imitation of the way the whole of the Son and the whole of the Spirit are given by the Father. We can therefore give back only the very gifts we have from the one we hope to pay. All our gifts to God take on the character of Eucharist offerings; we offer up to God the bread and wine that are already God's gifts to us as creator, empowered to do so by gifts already received in Christ. Finally, an adequate return seems out of the question when gifts are offered to fallible and sin-prone creatures. We are always giving back in a lesser form what God gave to us: the goods are always damaged to some degree or other by fallible and sinful creatures.[43] Giving for the sake of a good return would hardly make a lot of sense here. What, indeed, is the point of a return to God at all, if God is always going to get back less than God put out, if the gifts are always going to come back in poor condition?

God's purpose in giving is to benefit creatures, and therefore the proper return for God's giving is not so much directed back to God as directed to those creatures. A proper return here is one in which God's gifts both do the creatures who receive them good and are used for the good of others. A proper return displays what the gifts of God are good for: furthering the creatures' own good. A proper return in this way just demonstrates or puts into effect God's intent in giving them: creatures become the ministers of divine benefit, givers as God is in this sense, with the same goal of benefiting the recipients of God's gifts.

This return is what God expects without, as I have said, requiring it of us as a condition of God's giving to us. Rather than being obligated by what we have received from God, this return is just an appropriate response to the reception of gifts that benefit creatures.[44] It would be odd to say, for example, that the gift of a delicious meal for twelve obligates your eating it and sharing it with eleven friends; that is just an appropriate response to what it is. There is no external constraint being placed on the recipient; this response emerges from the recipient's own reaction to the gift, from what the gift means to the recipient. If a return to the giver seems the right thing to do, that is not because of a condition placed on the transaction, because this was the deal going into an exchange that began with the gift's being handed over to you, but because of what the gift is, how good it is. The gift's goodness is what inclines one to affirm that fact, to thank the one who brought it, to praise and honor the giver for her kindness and generosity. One doesn't make a return like that to the giver because one has to, but out of a free and joyful testimony to what one has received from another's hands. The more unconditional that giving was—the giver had no prior relationship with you, the giver could have avoided having anything to do with you, you hadn't done anything for them, and so on—the more wondrous the sense of gratitude and joy.

God may not be demanding a return for what God has given, but it is perfectly possible for unconditional giving to set up an obligation of return from the recipient's side: what the giver is demanding and what the recipient feels may be quite different.[45] The analogy of parents and children may be helpful here. Loving parents may give unconditionally to their children: they do whatever they can to benefit them right from the start, before they are even born and however rotten they turn out to be. Loving parents give for the benefit of their children even when no return to the parents is a possibility: say, when a child has a brain injury and loses the capacity to recognize them or ever act on their behalf. The more unconditional the giving here, the more the children will feel something approaching a strict obligation to give back to their parents, to switch roles with them in effect, when the time is right or circumstances warrant it: the children have resources of their own with which to benefit their parents, and their parents are in need—say, elderly, in poor health, and on a fixed retirement income. This sense of obligation is especially strong when one's parents are in a bad way because of what they did for you; for example, they face poverty in old age because of what they spent for your college tuition or for your hospital care as a child. But in the relations between God and us, nothing can ever happen to warrant such a role reversal: God is never put in the situation of needing anything from us; there is never anything that we have and God doesn't.

Especially in a case like this, when there is nothing one can do for the giver, one might very well think that the proper return is just to further the enterprise of giving that benefited you. One would testify in that case to the goodness of the gifts received from God by acting on them, by developing their beneficial qualities, for oneself and others, becoming thereby a giver as God is in turn. Again, this would be a kind of spontaneous reaction to the character of the gifts and not the consequence of one's having had to subordinate or align one's will to what the giver wants from you.

God's gifts are not put forth in any way that would demand or coerce a response from their recipients: often they don't even appear to be gifts. The typically hidden character of God's giving interrupts any demand for a response; it ensures that the response is unforced. If we are the gifts of God from the bottom up, we are not aware of having received them. These gifts efface themselves in their very occurrence by virtue of their difference from any other sort of gift exchange among creatures with which we are familiar—in which gift giving is never total, never responsible for the existence of the gifts' very recipients in their entirety. God's act of giving is invisible; what we see is the fact of it, its issue in created goods, which appear therefore to be simply our own.

God offers God's gifts almost unapparently, in a still small voice that might easily be overlooked. God doesn't appear in majesty to give the gifts of God to human beings in Christ. All one sees is a human being—and a poor and condemned one at that—who in the shape of his human living exhibits the gift-giving operations of God for the sake of the world. God doesn't blow all the bells and whistles to draw attention to what God is doing here: "look at all the great things I'm doing for you in Christ." Instead, God works among the least in the quietest of ways, in the failures of the world; that God was doing great things for us in Christ becomes at all obvious only after the fact, in forms of benefit—changed ways of living, the gift of immortality—that were hitherto beyond our reach.

God wants a return from us of a particular sort—our love and gratitude and devotion to God's mission of giving to others—and there is nothing especially problematic about that: God's unconditional giving is perfectly compatible with it. God gives unconditionally, whatever happens, to enable such a return. Benefiting others is the end of God's giving, and whether God too might be benefited in some incredibly attenuated sense of "benefit"—our weak chorus of praise drowned in the already fulsome radiance of God's glory—cannot be considered a corruption of God's beneficent motive, since God gives regardless. If God gets God's way and we make a proper return, the unconditionality of God's giving is unaffected; that unconditionality just means that God gives whatever the case may be, to further that end.

God doesn't refuse our gifts and need not do so in order to protect that unconditionality. It is a mistake to collapse giving whether or not there is a return into giving that has no return. The fulfillment of God's unconditional giving—giving that remains faithful to the effort to benefit us whatever happens—is our making a proper response. Far from forbidding a return, God graciously accepts back the gifts of that proper response. God accepts them, indeed, so as to return them to us, refreshed and renewed, elevated beyond our imagining. Again think of the Eucharist here. God graciously accepts the offerings we make in gratitude, however modest they might be—a little bread and wine—and returns them to us as Christ's very own body and blood, for our eternal sustenance. God doesn't use God's lack of need and prior fulsomeness to scorn our gifts or to highlight their failings. God's giving does not then humiliate us or work to keep us in an inferior's position of debt. God in giving to us does not bring about our debilitating dependency upon God;[46] God does not in that sense seek to give unilaterally, to be the only real giver. God is, instead, eager for us to become givers in turn and is doing everything possible to make that happen.

Universal Giving
The unconditionality of God's giving implies the absolute inclusiveness of God's giving: God gives without restrictions to everyone and everything, for the benefit of all. This is a second principle that makes a theological economy of grace distinctive. Because it has no preconditions, because there is nothing before it to condition it, God's giving as creator is universal in scope; everything that exists benefits. God's giving for the salvation of the world in Christ is also universally inclusive—the whole world is to benefit—for similar reasons: the gift of salvation in Christ has no conditions; there is nothing we must do or be in particular in order for God to be giving to us in Christ. In Christ God is clearly the gift-giving God of sinners as well as the righteous, of the Gentiles who lack God's gift of the covenant as well as the Jews who have the benefit of the law, of the suffering as well as the fortunate, indeed the God especially of the former in that they are the ones in greatest need of God's gifts. The distinction between good and bad, between Jew and Gentile—all the distinctions that typically determine the boundaries of human love and concern—fall away in that God gives simply to those in need, in order to address every respect in which they are needy, without concern for anything they especially are or have done to deserve it. In Christ not just the goods of created existence but the very fullness of God's own goodness are offered to the world without restriction: one simply has to be a creature, in need of what God has to offer; all creatures by definition, since they are not God, exhibit that need.

God's giving indeed breaks all the usual boundaries of closed communities of concern. In creating the world, God goes outside of God to offer gifts to the stranger, to what is not divine. God offers the gift of God's own self in partnership with a people by choosing those who are deprived and enslaved strangers within the community in which they reside. Jesus aligns himself with those without favor or good standing within the community of God's people and brings all within the very life of the triune God despite all their differences, despite indeed the greatest difference of all that nonetheless remains, the difference between divine and nondivine.

Giving back to God by furthering God's giving would have to involve, then, a respect for the common right of all to the goods of God, simply as creatures. Since the goods of creation—for example, being and well-being—are not offered just to particular creatures but to all of them, recognizing that one holds those goods as the gifts of God means recognizing God's efforts to give similarly to all others. The gifts of God's grace as creator amount in this way to an inclusive property right to life and all the goods of life, more or less as Locke defined it. But now, because this inclusive or common right is grounded in a principle of unconditional giving, nothing can stand in the way of a common right of access becoming a common right to actual possession and enjoyment. Unlike what Locke says, rights of individual appropriation cannot, for example, be made conditional upon work; legitimate possession by individuals must be based primarily on one's simple status as a creature in need.

This common possession right means that one should not hold one's property in a primarily exclusive way, guarding it against infringement by others. The right one is exercising to enjoy one's life and livelihood is what is to be shared with all others and not held against them or withheld from them. Your concern is not so much to keep others from what you have, as to see to it that everyone is enjoying what you are. Exclusive possession as a negative, protective right against others is only at issue as a secondary, reactive measure to reinstate common possession rights. A negative right would come into effect, for example, against those whose possessiveness deprives others of their common possession right, so as to enlarge the circle of those gifted with the goods of God. The vision of appropriation here is not accordingly individualistic. The way God's giving is to be realized by us, and not just God's intent, is communal or common. Individuals are to benefit only within a community in which all do so. The primary gift of God, one might say, is not held by individuals; it is a gift directly to community. God's primary gift is the gift of a particular sort of community, one without boundaries and organized so as to make common possession rights a reality, a community in which common possession rights are the social priority, a community dedicated to the well-being of all, without exception.

This common possession right that all people have simply as creatures puts those trying to further God's mission of giving under the obligation of helping them realize it. God's giving is not owed to creatures, but if those gifts are being given unconditionally by God to all in need, creatures are in fact owed the goods of God by those attempting to serve God's ends, without being or having done anything in particular to deserve them. Our good works, in short, are not owed to God, but they are to the world. This is an unconditioned obligation to give on our part because God's unobligated or gracious giving to the world is unconditioned by any differences of merit; God's giving only follows need, to the end of a complete distribution of the goods of God to all.

Those in need have a rightful claim on others, who are to be the ministers of divine beneficence to them, in imitation of the way the Son and the Spirit have by rights of nature what the Father nonetheless gives to them. On an equal footing with the Father, the Son and the Spirit already are by nature what they are given by the Father. In this sense they have by rights of nature what they are given; they are given what is their very own. Humans assumed by the Word in Christ, though in the needy situation of sin, have by rights of nature the gifts bestowed on them by virtue of their being the Word's very own. Though creatures are never owed anything by God—God's gifts are nothing but gracious here—God's decision to give them everything means an oddly analogous coming together of gift and right. We are to give to them what they have a right to; what they lack insofar as they are needy is their due. Because of God's unconditional beneficence, need determines a right here; we are only giving the needy their due when we try to meet their needs.

The community of concern to human beings as the ministers of divine benefit should therefore be as wide as God's gift-giving purview. In this universal community, humans should try to distribute the gifts of God as God does, without concern for whether they are especially deserved by their recipients. Without bothering themselves, for example, with distinctions between the "deserving" poor and the "undeserving" poor, human beings should give their full attention, instead, to the various needs of members of this worldwide community. They must offer special protections, moreover, as these become necessary, to those most likely to be left out of the community of concern at any point in time—the outcasts and strangers in their midst.

Again in imitation of God's relations with us, one gives to others with the hope that these gifts will be the basis for their activity as ministers of divine beneficence; one gives to them for their empowerment as givers in turn. Their failure to be such givers is not, however, cause for the forfeiture of those benefits. Gifts to them were not conditional on such a return; the absence of that return is therefore no grounds for discontinuing benefits. Their becoming ministers of divine beneficence by way of our gifts is not, moreover, to be considered a return under threat, a payment of a debt, or the meeting of an obligation. It is rather to be hoped for as the natural outcome of the joyful development of such gifts in thanks for gifts received. One expects dedication to the good of others to arise from the grateful sense that one has already been the recipient of benefit.

Noncompetition in a Community of Mutual Benefit

The reasonableness of such hopes gains support when the economic logic of a community dedicated to addressing the needs of all is further specified by a principle of noncompetitive relations that God's gift-giving abides by. So specified, unconditional giving in human relations to meet the needs of all takes on the shape of a community of mutual fulfillment.

Without this understanding of noncompetitive relations, the economy of grace might seem to require the superhuman, heroic efforts of isolated individuals. It might seem to require saints, with an utterly generous, unself-concerned love for others supremely uncommon in a world of sin and deprivation. Where giving back is not demanded from others and one gives regardless, what is to prevent one's own life from going down the drain? Mustn't that sort of awful outcome be the constant fear against which one battles? How can one expect people to give to others unconditionally in a dog-eat-dog world where every advantage offered to another is liable to be turned against them? Even where common possession rights are the norm, what is to stop a constant tug of war over possessions from breaking out in a world of scarce resources? Even when one recognizes that what one holds is a gift from another, how can one help clasping it to oneself in a possessive and defensive way against others, whose enjoyment of it will lessen yours? A very unrealistic demand will have to be placed on individuals to resist all this; the whole weight of the economy of grace will fall on the dispositions and attitudes of hapless individuals, unless that economy is structured in fundamentally noncompetitive ways. Noncompetitive relations are necessary to set up a social structure that encourages unconditional giving to others. In an economy organized noncompetitively the only sensible thing to do is to give unconditionally to others without regard for a return; that sort of giving now pays, rewards for it having simply been built into the way the system works.

Noncompetitive relations mean the following more specifically: First, there is no competition in property or possession. Something can be my property at the same time as it is another's; my having something in my possession need not lessen the degree to which it is in another's. Second, there is no competition between having oneself and giving to others. Giving is not to come at one's own expense; it is not self-sacrificial, in short. And my having is not at any one else's expense; to the contrary, it enables my giving to them for their good. These noncompetitive relations between having and giving develop the implications of noncompetitive forms of property and possession.

What one gives remains one's own property and possession because gift relations in a theological economy are not in any usual sense exchanges or transfers. Unlike goods that are bartered, traded, or sold, unlike the pure gifts on the contemporary Western understanding of that, gifts here are not being alienated—taken out of the possession of one party and handed over to others in ways that make them no longer the property of the first party. Nor, as in inalienable loans or noncommodity gift exchange, do gifts remain your property while being transferred out of your possession and into the possession of others; one doesn't, in other words, retain the property rights to things while losing use of them. And the degree to which you enjoy the use of them is not lessened by your giving others the use of them. Nothing is transferred, as if these gifts involved the moving of material goods from one site to another, and therefore one can retain full possession of one's own property in giving to others.

One sees this lack of competitive exchange or transfer, for example, in God's creating us. The conditions for competitive transfer are lacking for very peculiar reasons here. There is nothing to us prior to God's giving to receive such a transfer of possession or delivery of property. No one is home, so to speak, to take delivery; no one exists prior to God's giving to take the gift in hand. We as a whole are the gift, rather than being the gift's already existing recipients. And in creating us, God is not portioning out or alienating God's own property to us, but originating from the ground up, out of nothing, a distinctly created, nondivine version or reflection of the goodness that God retains in full.

But the usual theological reason for the absence of competitive sorts of transfer or exchange (the reason that underlies even their absence when God creates us) is that there is no need for them. What one has becomes the other's own, without the need for any transfer that would lessen your ownership or possession of it, because of a closeness in relationship to that other. Others are attached to, or one with you, and you to them. And therefore what you have becomes theirs, and what they have becomes yours. As the father says in the parable of the prodigal son: "Son, you are always with me, and all that is mine is yours" (Luke 15:31).

One can think of this "with" in either a physical or a personal and moral sense; the terms here—closeness, attached to, one with, and so forth—have multiple associations in that way. Think of a lit blowtorch set next to a lead pipe; by virtue of their physical closeness, the pipe gains the basic properties of the flame, without the flame losing them to any extent—the flame still burns, for example, at the same temperature. Or think of a closeness of personal identification or intense political solidarity, which need not have anything to do with physical proximity. In that case, the sufferings or doings of others might also be felt as one's own; what happens to others or what they do becomes a part of one's own story as well. Or think of a moral or legal relationship: crimes that others carry out might be attributed to you; they become your own in a legal or moral sense that obligates your making restitution for them, too, because of your identification with the group that committed them.

Analogies of both personal and physical closeness like this figure heavily in theological cases of noncompetitive property and possession. The persons of the Trinity share all the qualities that make God God because there is no separation in the way they are related to one another. Their relationship is so close that it is like three overlapping suns, burning together indissolubly. What the Father has the Son and the Spirit also have, because in them the very same thing repeats itself in different modes. The persons of the Trinity therefore only give to one another what they have and hold in common.

In Christ what humanity has becomes the Word's own and the reverse. This time not because the very same concrete thing is repeated in different modes but because the Word assumes to itself, unites with, becomes one with what is so very different from itself—the humanity of Jesus suffering under the sins of the world. Through the Word's identification with the humanity of Jesus, the Word acquires all the property of that humanity, appropriates it, so to speak; it now belongs to the Word as much as it belongs to that humanity. All that the humanity of Jesus accumulates over the course of his life—all that accrues to the humanity of Jesus by virtue of what he does and suffers—one can also now say that the Word does and suffers. Because all that happens to that humanity is in this way its shared or common property, the Word is able to give the gifts of its own property to that humanity. For example, the immortality that the Word continues to enjoy is given to that suffering humanity of Jesus so as to raise it up, resurrected and healed. To summarize what is going on here in the way Paul does in 2 Corinthians 8:9: by becoming one with us in Christ, the Word, while remaining rich, acquires our poverty and neediness, for the purpose of giving to us what we as mere creatures do not have or own by nature—the very riches of God's own life, its holiness and incorruptibility.

Just as the general pattern of noncompetitive property and possession looks a bit different depending on whether one is talking about the Trinity or Christ, so will this same pattern take a distinctive form in relations among human persons. In contrast to the relationship in Christ between a divine Word that is absolutely rich and a humanity ever poor in what divinity has to offer, in human society everyone is bound to be only relatively rich in some respects and relatively poor in others. The roles of giver and recipient could therefore properly shift back and forth depending upon the particular goods of human life involved; one would be talking in that case about persons establishing relationships of common property for the purpose of their mutual fulfillment in community. And unlike the case of the unsurpassable good of Jesus' own divinity, the goodness of gifts in human relations could presumably build as what everyone does with them for their own good is shared among givers and receivers: Gifts are enhanced as they are used by others for their own good and thereby enrich the givers; my enjoyment of what I have and give to others grows as theirs does. But the very basic shape that noncompetitive property and possession takes in the relation between humanity and divinity in Christ would still hold in relations among human persons. Identifying with others in a joint pursuit of universal benefit, those who are rich (in certain respects) should make the poverty of others (in those same respects) their own property; they should consider the poverty that others suffer to be something that is happening to them. The point of so closely identifying with others in their poverty is just to make, in turn, the good things one richly has the property of those poor in them, so as to alleviate their poverty. The lives of the poor are to be materially transformed by their being able to draw upon, as their very own property, what one continues to enjoy. The result is the possession and enjoyment of the very same goods in common: what we have for our own good is also the property of others from which they too benefit. We all benefit from the same things at the same time with the same right; the goods are at that point no more mine than yours.

More like the case of the Trinity than the case of Christ, in noncompetitive property and possession among humans the goods that are the natural properties of the givers are also natural to the recipients, since all the parties are human. But the greater similarity remains here, not with the Trinity, but with the relations between humanity and divinity in Christ. Like what happens in Christ, one takes to oneself what is different from oneself, one makes one's own, for example, those lacking what one has, for the specific purpose of alleviating their need. One is making a gift to them only if they don't already have what you are offering to them, in contrast to what happens in the case of gift-giving within the Trinity. There, in the Trinity, one person makes a gift to the others in the sense of its being superfluous to them, something that they don't need, a kind of redundancy. One doesn't have in human relations that self-sufficient communing of same with same that the common property of the Trinity suggests. In keeping with the universal community of unconditional giving, when one gives, one has everything to do with what is unlike oneself—those who are not in one's own circumstances, not in one's same economic class or social bracket. Gift relations are not established with those who already have what you have in terms of similar customs, a shared corporate group, family allegiance, or national affiliation, and so on, but with those who don't. As a gift giver you identify yourself very closely with all those you would not naturally resonate with or feel sympathy for because of their cultural and social differences from you.

To get a little better sense of what noncompetitive property and possession might be all about, let's come at the idea from the other way around, from the side of the recipient of gifts rather than from the side of the giver. We have what we have only in a relationship with those who are giving it to us, and therefore our property is always theirs too; having those things for one's own does not make them less the property and possessions of these others. This is true of what creatures have from God. Creatures have their own existence and qualities, it is true, as a kind of exclusive property in that what they have is natural to them and not to God: what they have is proper to them insofar as they are finite, and God is not finite. But all this property which is ours as creatures in this very strong sense is never simply ours in that it remains inseparable from God's giving of it. God's giving is never a finished fact, with an end product that goes its own way, giving completed in the given. Instead, we remain constantly dependent upon God for all that we are and have as creatures. We exist and have what we have as creatures only as God continues to hold all this up into existence, so to speak, only to the extent that God continues to give us all those things. In a new twist on the same general pattern, we genuinely have the gift of eternal life in Christ—it is ours to enjoy— but not in and of ourselves as some kind of new "supernatural" human property that we have acquired for ourselves. Eternal life, as a divine property, just cannot become a natural property of human beings in that way. We have eternal life only insofar as we are one with Christ, in a close relationship with him that allows us to draw upon what is proper to Christ as the divine Word incarnate. In sum, our coming to be and to act independently of God is never the ground (as it was for Locke) of our becoming ourselves and making things our own. We are our own and have for our own only as what we are and have remain God's own.

In this noncompetitive understanding of things, being ourselves as the persons we are and having all that we have for our own good should not come, then, at the expense of our being other peoples' own in community with them. Son and Spirit are themselves and all that they are for the good because they are the Son and the Spirit of the Father, and the reverse. We are ourselves, and have all that we have for the good as creatures, only to the extent we continue to be the triune God's creatures, ever receiving from the Father's hands of Son and Spirit. What the humanity of Jesus has, beyond its created capacities, is its own only as the Word makes that humanity the Word's own by assuming it to itself. What we have in Christ for our perfection and elevation becomes our own only as we are Christ's. Similarly, our lives as individuals should be constituted and enhanced in their goodness as we share our lives with others in community, identifying ourselves thereby as persons in community with others and not simply persons for ourselves. We perfect one another in community as our efforts to make the most of our own gifts and talents enter into and supplement the similar efforts of others in a combined venture for goods otherwise impossible.

Ideas about property in one's person are undercut in this way. You are owned by others who give all that you are—both what you have and your very person—to you, as your own, in order to benefit you. The artificial distinction between ourselves and our capacities, as in the capitalist understanding of property, is no longer necessary to make it seem as if one can keep something safe from the potentially hostile inroads of others in competitive markets for labor. Unlike what happens in those competitive capitalist relationships of ownership, if others own you here just by giving yourself to you and giving you everything you have for your good, then you are only more yourself for your own good the more you are owned by others—lock, stock, and barrel. One need not fear the fact that one is owned by these others—as if they might do what they please with you, as if they might take from you or restrict your good—since they own you only insofar as, respecting your differences from them, they give you to yourself in ways that advantage you. If they don't respect those differences and don't advantage you, they void their ownership of you, leaving you now in exclusive possession of yourself, with rights of self-protection against them. Holding one's person in a noncompetitive property relation with others in this way brings with it a secondary, derivative exclusive right of self-protection against those who would harm you.

When one accepts one's ownership by others, one's sense of self is expanded beyond anything simply one's own. One includes others, incorporates them, so to speak, within one's sense of self (which doesn't mean confusing them with oneself—any more than God and the human are to be confused in Christ). One does so out of a recognition that the life one lives is essentially constituted by relations with those others, to one's own benefit. One thereby comes to identify with others in the way that noncompetitive forms of property and possession require from givers. Knowing that we have ourselves as gifts from God and from all those others in whom we are in a community of mutual benefit, we now give to others, rather than withhold from them, by holding what we have simply as our own.

These noncompetitive forms of property and possession mean that giving to others and having oneself are simply not in competition with one another in a theological economy. Giving to others does not get in the way of having for oneself; having for oneself is not diminished by giving to others. For example, the persons of the Trinity give to one another without suffering loss, because each continues to have what it gives to the others in a noncompetitive form of possession. The Father does not empty himself of what he is in giving to the Son, only to be filled up again by a gift from the Son that returns what the Father originally gave away. A return from the Son is not necessary to cover the costs that the Father accrues in giving to him; the Son does make a return to the Father of what the Father gave him, but the Father doesn't suffer in giving to the Son apart from that return. The persons of the Trinity instead spill over into one another, as a resplendent light or ever bubbling fountain would, without self-evacuation or self-loss, so as to mirror one another in what they have and not in what they have lost to, and require back from, one another. Similarly, what the triune God gives to us does not decrease to any extent or in any fashion the therefore completely inalienable fullness of God's own life. God's giving to us may not be conditional upon our making a proper return to God—in fact we usually do not make a proper return—but it is therefore not a self-sacrificial giving. One can also make the 2 Corinthians passage mentioned earlier a key to the reading of Philippians 2:6-8: "[Jesus,] though he was in the form of God, did not regard equality with God as something to be exploited, but emptied himself, taking the form of a slave, being born in human likeness. And being found in human form, he humbled himself and became obedient to the point of death—even death on a cross." On that reading, it would not seem correct to say that the Word empties itself of its divinity in becoming a poor human being—though that act surely is empty of all pride and envy, a supreme act of unforced humility. The Word instead becomes human by acquiring humanity—by adding something, so to speak, to its own store of possessions—and not by giving up its own divinity, giving it away. What Jesus does for us—die on a cross—does not come at his own expense either, but is part of the process of perfecting his own humanity to glory; on the cross, mortality and the effects of sin are in the process of being overcome in Jesus' own life. We are to receive perfected humanity from Jesus as someone who enjoys it before us; our humanity will be perfected only to the extent his is already.

Following the same theological principle of noncompetition in our case, too, giving to others should not mean the impoverishment of ourselves. Though we are not ourselves as an exclusive possession, though we are not only our own, neither are we dispossessed in giving to others—self-evacuated, given away. In human relations, as elsewhere in a theological economy, giving should not be at odds with one's continuing to have. Reciprocity of giving would certainly ensure this. In a human community where others are not holding their gifts simply for themselves, presumably what one gave away would come back to one from others. But reciprocity is not required to prevent self-sacrifice in giving here.[47] Noncompetitive property and possession will do. What one gives remains one's property and possession and that is why giving does not come at one's own expense; one isn't giving by a giving away that might leave one bereft.

A community conforming to this idea would be a community of mutual fulfillment in which each effort to perfect oneself enriches others' efforts at self-perfection. One perfects oneself by making one's own the efforts of others to perfect themselves, their efforts, too, being furthered in the same way by one's own. Something like that is happening all the time in community living, but it is rarely made a major principle of community reform and self-purification.

Rather than being in competition with our benefiting others, having becomes in this way the very condition of our giving to others. Having does not stand in the way of and is not incompatible with giving to others; having need not, therefore, come at the expense of others. As elsewhere in a theological economy, we are to give to others not out of our poverty but out of our own fullness. Jesus entered into our poverty for the sake of the poor, but he did so as someone rich with the Father's own love. We do not give of our poverty but of what we have already received for our good so as to work for the good of others in response to their need. It is not as the poor that we are to give to others but as those rich, to whatever extent we are, giving to those poor in what we have, in solidarity with them. Efforts to realize one's own perfection, therefore, need not be at odds with concern for the needs of others. Self-concern is not at odds with that, just to the extent one's own perfections are what enable gift giving to others.

Without the danger of losing what we have by giving, we are freed up to give to others. The first person of the Trinity need not begrudge the second and third anything; the triune God need not begrudge the world anything; the Word need not begrudge the humanity of Jesus anything; Jesus need not begrudge us anything. And neither need we begrudge others: what we have for our own good others might have as well.

Making what one has the root and impulse of giving to others is simply the summary story of God and the world on my telling of it. The triune God is a God that communicates the goodness of the dynamic go-round of God's own life outward in love for what is not God. The whole point of God's dealings with us as creator, covenant partner, and redeemer in Christ is to bring the good of God's very life into our own. Our lives participate in that divine mission and thereby realize the shape of God's own economy by giving that follows the same principle: self-sharing for the good of others.

3

PUTTING A THEOLOGICAL ECONOMY TO WORK

The last chapter tried to use a theological economy to expand our economic imaginations as far as possible. That meant rereading the Christian story in ways that would allow for the greatest possible contrast between the principles of theological economy and those of capitalist exchange. Such a strategy might seem, however, to have doomed to practical irrelevance the theological economy so constructed. Theological economy seems a singularly peculiar, wild, and unworkable ideal. It is very hard to conceive in practical terms how this theological economy would work, just because it doesn't correspond to anything with which we are already familiar. It is simply very hard to picture what any of these theological principles might mean concretely. The sharp contrast between theological economy and any economy we know seems sufficient in and of itself, moreover, to dampen any promise of theological economy for today's world. Theological economy on my understanding of it appears to have nothing to do with the present structures of global capitalism and therefore to be offering a utopia: a proposal for no place and no time of our reckoning, a proposal that must remain in the imagination, limited to an imaginary world.

Inapplicable to a world like ours, which runs on very different presuppositions, theological economy would in that case be sterile in its opposition to it. It would leave the world to its own devices, without practical counsel for realistic change from a radically alternative viewpoint. Its only advice would be the complete overhaul of the present system, the simple replacement of the present system with a wholly different one following the lines of theological economy. And should the idea of a theological overhaul prove even more fanciful in today's world than the overthrow of global capitalism by a resurgent socialist or communist world economy, there seems nothing to do but hide out and hold out. We had better retire to, and tend the gardens of, those local self-sufficient economies that have managed to keep the forces of global capitalism at bay or have simply been overlooked by it in its rush for profit. We can wait there for the present system to destroy itself and for a new one to be born from its ashes and waste.[1]

Just as the utopian character of a theological economy would leave the world to its devices, such an economy might appear in that case to be thrown entirely on its own resources to generate, apart from the workings of the present system, a viable economic alternative.[2] With nothing to gain from attention to the capitalist system it hopes to escape, theological economy might limit its purview to the Bible or to church practices, and model its self-reliant, small-scale communities on, say, the subsistence agrarian economies of ancient Israel or on the desert monasteries of the early church, withdrawn from a world in which hope has been lost. Pretending to self-sufficiency, an alternative theological economy might in this way cut itself off from any sophisticated economic analysis of the realities of today's world—a sophisticated analysis of the real problems and potentials for change in the economic situation we now face, as the best academic disciplines of the day describe them.

But as I suggested in the first chapter, a theological economy, no matter how oppositional, is always formed in response to, in a kind of vis-à-vis with, the economy it contests. It only shows its meaning concretely, then, by being put into point-by-point conversation with what it opposes. When figuring out its practical import, isolated attention to the theological, and lack of reference to the complex workings of contemporary capitalism, only serve to make theological economy seem that much more of a will-o'-the-wisp.

Moreover, as I also suggested in the first chapter, the distinctiveness of a theological economy is not bought by respecting the boundaries of the economy as it is presently constituted, leaving it in peace to define its own course. Theological economy encroaches on and enters within the territory of the economy it opposes for the purpose of transforming the operations of that field. Theological economy does not linger on the outskirts of the economy, waiting for it to die a natural death, but works from within it, to turn or convert it to different principles of operation. A theological economy in this way germinates or comes to flower on alien soil. Or to change that pastoral metaphor, it comes to life from within the belly of the beast, so to speak—at its very heart—generating a radically new form of economy from capitalism's own blood and breath.

The Challenge of a Theological Economy

Theological economy enters into the present configuration of global capitalism to transform it at those points where the two fields cross each other in conflict. Just where the capitalist economy is at work, it can be met head on by and find itself crossed in a clash with an alternative configuration of economic life running along very different lines. Theological economy and global capitalism are not parallel planes but fields that come together in struggle because of their different vectors, their movements in opposite directions—one moving up, so to speak, in the direction of life; the other moving down, in the direction of death.

Despite the root contrast of underlying principles—indeed, without needing at all to lessen that contrast—there are any number of points at which theological economy can latch or hook onto the present operations of global capitalism in order to meet it in struggle. These are what I call points of relevant intersection and intervention. Something about the workings of global capitalism hints at the principles of theological economy we have explored; these are points allowing an opening for theological economy. The hints might sometimes be positive intimations and at other times more like rifts or strains in the capitalist fabric—crises, cries for help really, in a world at capitalism's mercy—to be filled in uncommon fashion by what theological principles would direct. Either way, it is at these points that the workings of the present system might find themselves pushed in new directions, reworked to overcome truncated hopes, unrectified losses, callous exclusions, and winner-take-all competitive conflicts.

Realistic, practically viable theological proposals for changing the present system are generated, we'll see, out of these partial overlaps and clashes, as the theological principles of economy meet the workings of the capitalist system so as to infiltrate and subvert its usual operations. We are not left with the desperate sense of a failure of means, so typical of the modern zeitgeist in the West. Complex, decentralized networks of money and communication media make it very difficult in our world to analyze global problems in ways that clarify mechanisms for global change. Resisting any such trend of pessimistic defeatism, theological economy provides in this way not only, as the last chapter showed, a systematic vision of what to shoot for but some plan for getting from here to there.

In the process, theological economy challenges the common idea at the present time of the ineluctability of capitalism's current configuration. Global capitalism can be changed and redirected by human decision; it is not the immovable object or implacable juggernaut that neoliberal economists would like us to think it is. The shape of capitalism has never been the pure product of economic forces but always the precipitate of additional social and political forces working together or against one another to push it this way or that.[3] What would the capitalism of the second half of the last century be, for example, without the growth of labor unions? Or what would the capitalism of this century be apart from the dominance of the United States on the world scene?

Capitalism may inevitably fall into crises of its own making, but historically contingent political decisions are a decisive factor in any response.[4] For example, the Bretton Woods agreement of 1944, which was designed to prevent another Great Depression by establishing international regulatory bodies like the World Bank and International Monetary Fund (IMF), failed to follow through on the proposals of John Maynard Keynes that would have spread the burden of imbalances of trade to those with trade surpluses, in part because of pressure from the United States.[5] The debt crisis among developing nations in the early 1980s would have looked quite different without the election of Ronald Reagan, whose appointees almost single-handedly altered the policies of the International Monetary Fund and World Bank to favor the now much maligned policies of so-called structural adjustment for developing nations, which cost those nations their infrastructure and job growth.[6] The increase in worldwide trade that defines global capitalism and that resolved the "stagflation"—inflation with slow growth—of the 70s is in great part the product of political decision-making bodies at the international level—GATT (General Agreement on Tariffs and Trade) and its successor, the WTO (World Trade Organization). Another outcome is the growth in international finance: the free flow of money worldwide is the product of deregulation—that is, what prevents national states from keeping currency flows within their own borders.

One cannot say that the direction those political and social forces take is capitalism's doing, the ultimate product of the overriding influence of capitalism's own directives, since alternative paths are written into capitalism itself. For example, employers have the option of increasing profit margins by lowering wages or by increasing productivity. Their profit margins might remain the same either way; it is the social consequences of such decisions that markedly differ. Increased productivity may mean one needs less work from one's employees, but it remains on open question whether one should fire some or have them all work less. And so on. On the national level, it is public policy that decides whether the stability of the currency or full employment is the priority, whether financial investments are to be favored over productive ones, and so forth. In the former case, for example, the government through its fiscal and monetary policies might try to keep interest rates high, and in the latter case it might try to keep them low. Many argue that in the current global economic climate, international finance always trumps government efforts to increase employment through low interest rates and deficit spending; capital will flee those nations in search of higher returns, forcing them, in effect, to raise interest rates to try to attract it back. But this argument overlooks the fact that what has been deregulated can be re-regulated; a political decision remains to be made on the international level about the free flow of currencies across national borders when it comes at the expense of job creation worldwide. In short, there is always some room to maneuver within capitalism, different options that it is possible to pursue. Capitalism is essentially marked by internal strains that allow for different courses of action, to be decided by considerations, factors and forces, beyond its own sphere.

The result is a capitalism that takes different shapes.[7] Capitalism in Japan is not the same as capitalism in the United States. Both differ from what one finds in Germany, and all of these vary from the capitalism of the Scandinavian countries. Evidently up for grabs within the same basic structures of the present capitalist economy, and accounting for its changing face from place to place, are such matters as: the distribution of private and public sector employment, the degree of wage flexibility, the levels and sources of government funding, tax policy, focus on export or domestic markets, concern over inflation versus concern for job growth, the extent of government protection for and support of research and development within new businesses, and so forth. Add the combined effects of such national policy decisions to the influence of international regulatory bodies on the course of financial flows and world trade, and there is no reason to think that global capitalism cannot be budged from its present configuration.

The question for us then becomes what new face global capitalism might display as it is put under pressure from theological economy. How is it likely to be twisted and turned in their clashing conjunction? Let's begin to answer the question by looking at the most general points of intersection and intervention between a theological economy and global capitalism.

The Significance of Economic Interdependence

The overall understanding of a theological economy, as you remember, is of a universally inclusive system for the increase and distribution of goods, one dedicated to the well-being of all its members and organized to ensure that what benefits one benefits all. The global character of present-day capitalism would be a first very general point of intersection with this all-encompassing theological economy. The way that theological economy breaks the boundaries of closed communities seems to resonate with the enormous expansion of economic interdependencies in today's world, all those general features of capitalism that currently disrupt the self-sufficiency of every economic subgroup short of the global. These interdependencies now mark production, trade, and finance. Fueled by technological advances in transportation and communication systems, companies today are not simply multinational but transnational.[8] Companies do not, in other words, just set up plants in other countries (as they used to do in order, for example, to get around trade barriers) but parcel out the various components of the production process to quasi-independent subcontractors all over the world in order to take advantage of the various cost-cutting opportunities available there. Assembly plants, for example, can be located near consumer markets to cut down on transportation costs. The labor-intensive portions of the production process can be located where labor costs are low. And so on. World trade, particularly this sort of intra-product trade among companies working together in transnationally coordinated production processes, has increased exponentially, outstripping world production levels. The financing for this transnational production and increase in worldwide trade has also become transnational, in the sense that the core firms of these transnational networks of production are controlling the financing of their operations worldwide. But more significantly, finance capital has become transnational by being freed from productive investment altogether. One can now trade, for example, future earnings in the debts one is owed or trade currencies. At the touch of a button on a computer screen, billions of units of one currency can be sold for another. One any single day, the number of these foreign exchange transactions indeed dwarfs the volume of world trade. Transnational finance just means here that money is no longer under the control of the countries that print it.

A theological economy has a stake in the expansion of economic concern, so as to break the limits of bounded interests. The time and space compression, which new communication technologies make possible and which is the cultural correlate of such transnational socio-economic interdependencies, reduces the significance of geographical distance for the establishment of economic concern.[9] What happens in Asia is of almost as much concern to me as what happens next door to the extent that I cannot isolate myself and my more geographically proximate neighbors from the near immediate effects, in real time, of those geographically distant events. Despite the dominance in the theological literature on globalization of a call to return to local self-sufficient communities, it seems to me the interests of a theological economy have a clear point of intersection or overlap here with economic globalization—at least at this most general of levels.

The obvious question to ask here from the standpoint of theological economy is whether people are really benefiting across the board from these economic interdependencies. All that increased interdependency might mean here is increased cutthroat competition, which violates one of the major principles of theological economy developed in the last chapter. In that case, for example, what is happening to the wage levels of workers in Singapore is as important to me as the going rate for piece workers in the garment district of New York City where I work, because, for all the geographical distance, I am competing with them for my job. If their wage is appreciably lower, I am liable to lose mine. Especially if no taxes or environmental regulations apply to companies there, production might be moved, or these workers could migrate to New York City, bringing their lower wage expectations with them, and take my job out from under me. Presumably, everyone benefits in the long run from the ensuing lower prices for goods of this sort, whose production does not allow for the productivity increases of capital-intensive technological innovation and is therefore always dependent upon a lot of labor. But those low prices will not do me much good if I cannot pay for even inexpensive clothes because I am unemployed.

These are extremely serious issues, and I do not mean to minimize them. The economic interdependencies that make up global capitalism might indeed be a very mixed bag; reforms are necessary, as we will see, in all the economic sectors that make it up, with some much more amenable than others to reform of a mutually beneficial sort. Whether, for example, in these new circumstances of global mobility, unrestricted free trade can ultimately prove to be of mutual benefit to all trading partners, as the theory of comparative advantage would have it, has become so complicated a technical matter that I cannot, as a nonexpert, form a clear opinion about it.[10] There certainly appear to be ways, however, of making that trade more equitable in the short term, and lifting unfair barriers to trade—making trade freer—is, we shall see, much of what needs to be done. Free flowing finance capital, however, especially when it is de-linked from productive investment, is undoubtedly problematic in its essential aspects, as I'll show later in this chapter.

The real question from the standpoint of theological economy is whether solving such problems of cutthroat competition means retreat from global concern or its intensification. The structures of theological economy favor the latter form of response. Workers in Singapore remain my concern; I am concerned specifically about their benefit. The solution to competition from them that hurts me would therefore be an international labor movement to raise their wages. In similar fashion the response to wage-lowering pressure from illegal immigrants should not be measures to prevent their mobility but efforts to mobilize them in the usual worker agitation for increased pay levels and benefits. Immigration is discouraged not by quotas and high fences but by improving the job opportunities for people in their own countries.[11] International environmental regulations setting minimums for compliance by corporations everywhere would be a good idea. Taxes could be shifted elsewhere in the U.S. to enable the garment industry to stay here. But particularly in developed nations, which do not have an advantage over others in cheap labor, it simply makes better sense for taxes, whoever pays them, to be earmarked for retraining workers whose jobs have been lost to foreign competition, enabling them thereby to get better paying jobs in higher productivity industries—say, as software designers.

The point of general intervention, then, has to do with whether the present global system is, or ever could be, even in an approximate way, an economy dedicated to fulfilling the needs of all in a mutually beneficial way. Here the concerns of theological economy intersect with those economists and human development theorists who argue for a return of national and international concern for full employment and poverty reduction and for profit and growth that do not come at the expense of people and their ability to realize their capabilities.[12] Not all policies favoring economic growth lead to full employment and poverty reduction. One should, whenever possible, promote growth strategies in which the economy grows and poverty is reduced at the same time. Land reform is a case in point. Where a very few people own most of the land and sharecropping is the norm, those working the land have their economic incentives reduced by what amounts to a very large hidden tax on their agricultural efforts. Land reform, giving ownership of the land to those who work it, would therefore alleviate poverty at the same time as it would boost incentives to increased agricultural output.[13]

Indeed, not only the welfare effects of the current system but its truly global character can be disputed. International production, trade, and finance are limited in great part to already developed nations.[14] Transnational corporations do not employ people from every part of the world but from a limited sector, usually within the developed world.[15] What counts in capitalist employment is not people but their labor power; and that labor power is determined, for example, by how well educated, skilled, and healthy they are. Nations, particularly developing ones, are far from equal in such human resources.[16] International trade is, in turn, restricted, since the great majority of it is in the goods and services that make up the production processes of these same transnational corporations.[17] Finance capital, finally, tends to concentrate in the developed nations because the risks are lowest there.[18] Firms in developed nations tend, for example, to have proven track records and to enjoy greater productivity from technology-intensive capital investment than is true elsewhere. They are just safer bets. The result is that large areas of the world—for example, most of sub-Saharan Africa, rural and inner-city areas of the so-called developed world—find themselves excluded from the "global" system. These areas become for almost all intents and purposes economic dead-zones. Very little capital investment comes in; any surplus capital flows out to areas of the world where profit making is more assured. Next to nothing is bought or sold; few financial transactions (of a legal nature) occur there.

One can argue, moreover, that profit is generated within the current system by processes of relative exclusion, which systematically disadvantage the vast majority of even the people that global capitalism manages to encompass. Low-wage workers in many parts of the world are excluded from the consumer markets in the goods they produce; goods are produced solely for export and to a lesser extent for sale to national elites. At the same time, the majority of people in those consumer markets are progressively excluded from manufacturing the goods they buy, as production facilities shift to the lower-wage sites. Low-priced goods and profit generally are being generated off the backs of workers in all the countries in which transnational corporations operate, while high incomes are restricted to the few who are able, via information technologies, to participate in quite lucrative nonproductive financial exchanges such as currency trading, stock value speculation, and the buying and selling of a variety of highly complicated financial instruments (derivatives, securities, call and put options).

Only debtor nations pay, moreover, for the bad loans made to them —not the creditors who, awash in so-called Petro- or Euro-dollars since the 70s, have been extending loans profligately and unwisely, indeed often pressuring developing nations into taking them.[19] Creditors never have to take a loss or write off their bad loans. Debtor nations are not, for example, allowed to declare bankruptcy (the way individual people or corporations do) and thereby gain immunity from their creditors. And the International Monetary Fund in effect guarantees their pay back. International monetary policies for the two-thirds world—particularly, the structural conditions placed on international financial aid since the 80s—simply seem geared to ensuring the repayment of debt.[20] For example, as a condition for more international funds, high interest rates are set by the banks, and cutbacks in government spending tighten the money supply. These measures prevent inflation and stabilize the currency; loans thereby retain their value. But such restrictive monetary and fiscal policies also bring with them very high costs in domestic unemployment and the foregoing of infrastructure spending to meet even the basic needs of people for schools and roads, clean water, and human waste disposal. Production for export is encouraged and imports are curtailed not by trade restrictions, but by simple loss of domestic demand—few people can afford to pay for these imports any longer. In this way foreign currency reserves are built up with which to pay back foreign loans.

The result of this exclusive shouldering of their bad debt burden is a liquidity crunch among developing nations. They are so busy paying off their international debts that they don't have money for investing in domestic industries to compete with those of the developed nations. International money may flood in to seed investment, but it can just as easily run out again in the deregulated financial markets of today.[21] The recipients of this money in the developing nations are just as likely as anyone else to try to shift it to the safer havens of developed nations, out of their own countries and into, say, overseas productive investment opportunities or currencies.

Furthermore, unfair trade practices ensure that developing nations pay to rectify trade imbalances while developed nations do not.[22] Developed nations that run trade surpluses—that export more than they import—are not forced to increase their imports or have those surpluses canceled or rerouted to nations running trade deficits, as they would have been required to do, for example, under the original plans submitted by Keynes for the international regulatory bodies to be set up at Bretton Woods.[23] Indeed, developed nations routinely protect those industries that would suffer most from competition from developing nations, thereby curtailing sales of what developing countries have to export.[24] Agriculture and textiles, for example, are subsidized in developed countries; import tariffs or quotas are placed on clothing and raw materials coming into them from developing nations.[25] Developing nations, on the other hand, are required—for example, by IMF mandate—to increase their exports in order to lessen trade deficits. And they are not permitted, by stipulation of the WTO, to lessen those deficits by restricting imports through the imposition of tariffs or quotas.[26]

Given the fact that neither the burdens nor the benefits are shared, one can hardly say this is a system presently dedicated to meeting the needs of people everywhere and organized for the mutual benefit of all. The question is whether this is an intrinsic feature of global capitalism—perhaps even an intrinsic feature of capitalism period.[27] Or whether the system might allow for —even work better (in its own terms)—were it to move in the directions a theological economy suggests. Are the present conditions of global capitalism a recipe for crisis or simply the status quo for a system dedicated to profit and economic growth at other peoples' expense? If they are the makings of crisis, would the major reforms suggested by the principles of a theological economy be a solution? Might those reforms, indeed, prove a better fix than the usual capitalist ones, the sort of fixes typical of capitalism over its historical course, which many would argue simply generate new problems on a different scale?

These are very big and important questions, and we will have to return to them. But I would like to approach these questions by a gradual route. Rather than concentrate on the overall big picture drawn by theological economy, let's break all this down and concentrate on more specific points of intervention and intersection with global capitalism that hinge on the more specific, individual principles of theological economy making up the big picture. We have already in fact been exploring points of intersection and intervention with the more specific theological principle of inclusive economic community. But what about some of the other more specific theological principles I laid out in the last chapter, such as unconditional giving and noncompetitive possession and use, and under the latter, the even more specific sub-principles of giving without loss and benefit that does not come at the expense of others? What kind of hooks can be generated from these more specific theological vantage points?

Welfare and Unconditional Giving

Let's start with the theological principle of unconditional giving. One point of obvious intervention would be the decline of welfare provision in many national governments worldwide and the setting of conditions on welfare receipt—working in exchange for welfare benefits (so-called workfare), moral character tests, payments proportionate to one's contributions, and so on—the sort of conditions typically put on welfare in the United States. Why, to begin with, is this a feature of the new global economy? In the developing world, the hollowing out of state service provision seems the product in great part of conditions put on international monetary aid by the IMF. Restricted government spending is one way to prevent inflation and to encourage export trade by limiting domestic demand, period, for goods. The suspicion about such policies is, again, that they are primarily motivated by the concern for foreign debt repayment. Low inflation helps maintain the value of loans to these countries, while exports generate the foreign monetary reserves necessary to pay them back. In the developed world, the hollowing out of government services was in part a reaction in the late 70s to the competitive inefficiencies that Keynesian fiscal and monetary policies (big government and easy money) were supposed to have promoted. Tightened state fiscal and monetary policies were designed to increase competitiveness by flushing inefficiencies out of the system. But international competition for corporate investment and finance capital in the new global economy clearly also plays a significant role. Irresponsible fiscal policy—say, running huge deficits to pay for welfare provision—might scare off investors. Taxes on corporations to pay for a welfare state might incline them, in this now transnational economic world, to go elsewhere. A nation will succeed in attracting international financial flows only if its currency is stable, and that means cutting back on any public sector spending that risks increased inflation. Inflation lowers the value of one's currency and could lead to capital flight from it—for example, a massive sell off of it on international financial markets. This hollowing out also results from the increased disciplining of government policy by corporate interests, in a global economic situation in which corporations can threaten to move. The state is always torn between a need to remain popular among the general citizenry—a need that promotes welfare provision—and the state's dependence on economic growth for income generation via taxation—a concern that promotes government policies favoring corporate profit. Business is happy to divert capital from government into its own coffers by tipping the balance of the state's interests toward itself when it has the leverage. The benefit to business of a worker surplus—a benefit in the form of the low wages that it can pay its workers under those circumstances—also means that business interests converge with shrinking government employment roles and with a shift from welfare to workfare on the part of the state. Finally, the privatizing of services previously supplied by the state—education, transportation, and communication systems—helps to solve capital's over-accumulation problems. When demand is sluggish, there is something to do with surplus profit and underutilized production capacity.[28]

The theological principle of unconditional giving would intervene here to suggest welfare provision as a universal entitlement, sensitive only to need. Welfare provision should be considered a right of the needy, a matter of justice rather than a matter of voluntary largesse on the part of the privileged. In that case, distinctions between the deserving and undeserving become inappropriate measures for determining welfare provision. And gone thereby are all the debasing conditions for receipt of public assistance, the demeaning supervision and invasions of privacy.[29] The usual stigma of welfare is further diminished by the expanded sense of welfare according to universalistic principles. Everything that government expenditures add to your well-being constitutes welfare, and therefore everybody gets welfare in one form of another: you might not need cash assistance or food stamps and in fact might be too wealthy in retirement to require Social Security payments, but you still benefit from public parks, trash collection, unemployment insurance, and so forth.

Such theological support for fulsome welfare provision runs counter to present global trends, but it need not be fundamentally at odds with the demands of the new global economy. While making it conditional upon work is incompatible with the theological principle of unconditional giving, welfare provision should, in keeping with a theological stress on a community of mutual fulfillment, be sufficiently far ranging to enable recipients to make contributions to society commensurate with their full potentials. It should, in short, enable people to work at their highest levels of capacity, presumably some of the time at least, in better paying jobs. Welfare provision would include such things as monetary payments, education, and health care, all of which enhance the ability of recipients to develop their capacities in ways that might ultimately prove socially beneficial—that is, by enabling recipients to raise their children well, to enter the workforce as productive members of society, and to contribute to the artistic and cultural life of the community.

Welfare, and indeed government infrastructure provision generally, could in this way be viewed as instrumental to economic growth.[30] The populace of welfare states of this kind could be counted on to be creative and enterprising and the engine of new growth. Welfare provision would foster development, moreover, of the sort of healthy, educated, and skilled workforce capable of rapid adjustment to the technologically innovative industries typical of today's global capitalism. Such a workforce could only enhance economic productivity, and thereby aid and abet the sort of profitability without low wages that such technologically innovative businesses permit.

It is, indeed, the increased productivity of today's transnational business ventures, using post-Fordist production techniques to be discussed later in this chapter, that would help pay in the main for these extensive welfare provisions.[31] Businesses that remain in developed countries are, indeed, forced across the board into productivity gains by competition from developing countries, because they do not have the option of cutting costs by reducing wages to the levels found in developing nations.[32] Welfare provision in this sort of increased productivity business climate would be funded not by deficit spending but by growth.

Fear of deficits from welfare spending is in any case overblown—even disingenuous—for the case of the United States. The economic strength of the United States, along with the fact that the dollar remains the default currency for international capital transactions of all sorts, presently allows us to run enormous deficits caused by military spending (among other things), without suffering any particular ill effect from international financial markets. Even with a depressed currency from trade deficits and without high interest rates to attract international financial capital, there is no run on our currency. The re-regulation of financial markets to discourage capital flight is, moreover, as mentioned above, always a real possibility.

Taxation need not fall excessively on corporations in such a scenario of growth from high productivity industries. Increased rates of growth via productivity gains might cover the increased expenditures of welfare provision without raising rates of taxation on those corporations.[33] The tax burden, moreover, could be spread around. Highly productive technology-driven industries can afford to pay their workers more (and typically do); highly paid workers can afford to be taxed, via either their payrolls or their consumption.[34] The education and training supplied by extensive welfare provision might be expected to push people progressively into higher tax-bracket incomes. An enlarged public service sector would further expand the tax base.[35]

There is no evidence, furthermore, to suggest that workers and corporate executives choose to flee high taxes when such taxes bring with them a quality of life that increased incomes from low taxes cannot easily buy.[36] Your three-hundred-dollar tax cut simply cannot replace the beautiful public park or wonderful school system or well-maintained roads and transit systems that additional universal taxes of that amount might conceivably provide. The possibility of that sort of provision increases when tax revenues are used efficiently. Countries would be competing with one another to attract business primarily, then, not by progressively lowering the tax burden on corporations, but by their efficient use of tax revenues.[37]

Such efficient use of tax revenues—getting the most bang in benefits for your buck—might indeed mean a lessening of the overall tax burden. Taxes need not be high even with the universalistic benefits a theological economy promotes, since provision is sensitive to need. You are not entitled to a lot simply because you have contributed a lot, if you do not need the benefits.

Far from being incompatible with the new global economy, one could argue that increased welfare provision dovetails with it. The issue here isn't simply the way welfare provision supports and sustains the formation of a skilled workforce and creative business class. One can also argue that the flexible production techniques of today require a flexibility from workers that welfare provision enables. Profitability in today's capitalism requires rapid response to decreased demand and rapid shifts to new product lines. Generous welfare provision makes it easier for companies to hire and fire: doing so need not foment worker ire.[38] Welfare provision might also encourage the sort of lifelong learning that workers need to shift skills with changing markets over the course of their working lives. Moreover, if welfare provision extends as a universal right to lower-income working people, not just to those out of work, this in effect increases the international competitiveness of businesses in the developed world that cannot be made more productive and whose profitability remains dependent on worker pay scales. The wages they pay their workers can be lower without worker hardship with the difference made up by welfare benefits.[39] Finally, one might argue that the contribution welfare makes to social stability only becomes more important under global capitalism.[40] Business cycle fluctuations are likely to become only more extreme when financial capital is globally mobile: capital from all over moves very rapidly to the same likely sources of profit, leading to over-investment and over-expansion and just as quick capital flight. Global competition increases the risks to businesses—cheap imports undercutting the price of goods manufactured in the home country, jobs in one country lost to workers in another. Without welfare provision to lessen the hardships that people face as a result, social instability is a definite likelihood.

The common counter-argument to my association here of extensive welfare provision with productivity growth appeals to the supposed moral hazards of welfare. Disincentives to socially beneficial work are the purported products of welfare provision. The theory is that when people have, for example, generous unemployment insurance and health benefits, they perform sub-optimally on the job, call in sick more often, and delay the search for work. There is, however, very little statistical evidence to support these contentions.[41] Nations with the best welfare provision—say, Scandinavian countries—are often also the ones with the most productive work forces. They do not, moreover, have higher vacancy rates than other countries—more people out of work, for example, than one would expect from the jobs available.[42] The moral hazard argument indeed supplies a very dubious microeconomic explanation for macro developments. Ignoring the host of complex global forces that affect today's national economies, the explanation for nations becoming noncompetitive is simply their workers' laziness.

Psychological assumptions are what lend the moral hazard argument its plausibility, but these assumptions are rather easy to criticize. One might question, for example, whether socially beneficial work is motivated simply by fear of starvation or desire for economic gain, as the moral hazard argument presumes. Can we not also assume that personal satisfaction, accruing from the realization of one's talents, is (among other things) a significant motivator?

Even if psychological disincentives to productive work are sometimes produced by welfare provision, one can argue that there are psychologically plausible ways around them short of the big stick of loss of benefits. One can argue, for example, that such disincentives are the result of limiting welfare provision to money payments. When welfare provisions foster the realization of capabilities as well, such disincentives are discouraged. In other words, if you give nothing but money to people when they are out of work, they may be inclined to stay that way; if you also give them free education to gain new skills, public transport to the jobs they otherwise cannot get to, child care, or health care to overcome the medical problems that keep them bedridden, the result might be entirely different. In countries where, despite government supports like these for holding a job, workers are frequently absent due to illness, it has been found that more attention to the needs of workers, rather than less, is what improves things. Helping them address their health care needs (even providing on-site nurses and doctors), moving people to less physically demanding jobs, buying them special equipment to make performance of their jobs easier—all these measures that convince workers of their value to the company are what make the difference.[43]

Capitalist Competition and the Principle of Noncompetitiveness

Let's turn now to the theological principle of noncompetitiveness. Here we seem to have the principles of theological economy at their most utopian—at least if we presume, as I do for the most part, that capitalism is the only game in town for most purposes of efficient resource allocation and that capitalist market efficiency is all about competition. To prevent the appearance of sterile utopianism, all we need to do, however, is recognize the way certain noncompetitive features are built into capitalist principles; these noncompetitive features provide the hooks for theological intersection and intervention in this case.

There are two main sites for a principle of noncompetitiveness within capitalism. First, there is the capitalist ideal of a mutually beneficial competitive equilibrium, a real possibility that capitalist competition should always be circling around, at least if you believe Adam Smith. Second, there is the capitalist interest in avoiding mutually destructive economic spirals and in fostering complementary or virtuous ones. Let's take each in turn.

The first case puts the win/loss character of capitalist competition into perspective. Leaving Adam Smith aside for the moment, let's assume with Marxist theorists (as I did in the last chapter) that capitalist profit is always generated at the expense of labor. Profit, in other words, is always at root a matter of extracting more value out of one's workers than one pays them. This fundamentally competitive scheme does not exclude a mutually beneficial possibility. The optimal situation indeed is not one in which workers are paid next to nothing in order to maximize profit margins. Paying them next to nothing would not permit the workforce to be reproduced; that is, people would not be enjoying a sufficient quality of life to enable productive work in such a circumstance. And there would be no one with the money to buy the goods produced, particularly in the mass quantities, the economies of scale, required by capitalist production in most periods of its history. Contrary to such a pure win/loss scenario, it is possible, within this still fundamentally competitive situation between capitalists and labor, for labor to be paid more at the same time as the rate of extraction of value from labor, and thereby capitalist profit, increase.[44] Profit in that case is not only used for additional capital investment but passed onto workers for their benefit as well, the assumption being that healthier, happier workers are more productive ones and that increased pay means increased spending, thereby fueling demand for what one produces. As even Henry Ford knew very well, it is not a good idea to pay auto workers so little they cannot afford to purchase cars. The rate of extracting value from labor increases here because of productivity gains. The employer gets progressively more out of the same amount of labor by way, for example, of technological innovation. And therefore profit need not be generated by putting downward pressure on wages. As the theorists of the French Regulation School of economists inform us, capitalism can try to maintain itself under either extensive or intensive regimes of profit accumulation.[45] In the former case, profit is ensured by increases in productivity, and the tension between workers and management finds resolution in a positive-sum game: the more employers profit, the more workers gain. In the latter case, profit is generated by paying workers less, and relations between the two deadlock in a zero-sum game: employers gain only to the extent workers lose. The former scenario, for reasons already mentioned, is the better choice. By funding both worker productivity and increased demand, it has the greater long-term potential to stoke the engines of economic growth. It also avoids worker unrest by sustaining wage increases and lessening the potential for extreme income disparities between workers and their employers.

Let's turn now to competition among capitalists and a more Adam Smithian view of the market equilibrium that should result from it. According to Smith, perfect competition should lead to a situation where everyone benefits: all capitalists make some profit (the average rate), while consumers are able to buy the quality goods they want at the least possible cost. The win/loss character of capitalist competition occurs in the dynamic processes leading to and away from this state of equilibrium or mutual benefit. That is, capitalists are always trying to gain more than the average rate of profit. They could do that by lowering their costs somehow—for example, by paying their workers less or by technological innovation or by more efficient techniques for the operation of existing machinery. They could also try to increase their rate of profit by gaining greater market share or by taking advantage of existing inequalities of circumstance (say, by using the benefits of geographic location, the fact that production sites happen to be next door to consumer markets, to minimize transportation costs, or by using existing inequalities of political power to bargain for cheaper manufacturing inputs, and so on). These techniques for gaining more than the average rate of profit themselves involve win/loss forms of competition; no firm gains any competitive advantage here if all the other firms succeed in doing exactly the same thing at the same time. But, more important, these techniques also enable win/loss competition in the exchange market: they make it so that consumers will buy your product (because it is cheaper, of better quality, or both) and not your competitors'. In order to compete more effectively for such buyers, the other, now disadvantaged firms will be forced to try their hand at the same techniques for generating a greater profit margin—for example, they will have to modernize their equipment—or go out of business. When they do manage to do so successfully, the profit rate again stabilizes (at a higher average level than previously) across the industry with every firm making some profit (the new average rate) and with the consumer benefiting. Equilibrium, in short, is reestablished. And then the mechanisms of win/loss disequilibrium resume, with every firm trying to gain a greater than average rate of profit.

What is important to see for our purposes is that the overall competitive system disintegrates without the equilibrium point. In other words, a pure win/loss competition is not optimal even from a capitalist point of view. The disequilibriums that surround the generation of so-called super-profits (profits, that is, that exceed the average rate) should not be made permanent, even though it would seem to be in the interest of every individual firm benefiting from them to make them so. Making these disequilibriums permanent simply undermines the fundamental structures of capitalism. If other companies are prevented from catching up (or cannot catch up quickly enough) so that market equilibrium is ruled out, the system, in short, becomes noncompetitive. The company that is first to achieve the increased rate of profit will eventually have the field to itself; monopoly ensues, with the usual consequences of price rises, quality declines, and misallocation of resources away from the production of goods that people really want.

The theological principles of noncompetition and mutual benefit obviously intersect here with the capitalist interest in conditions favoring the possibility of recurrent market equilibrium. Theological intervention, in keeping with the theological principle of universal community, would respond to the fact that this concern for market equilibrium is not often applied globally, at least in any consistent way.[46] Certainly on a global level, conditions for competitive equilibrium are missing, in that the competitive advantages already enjoyed by developed nations seem to be becoming permanent. Capitalism always generates profit through differences in competitive edge, but the developed nations are taking advantage of existing systematic economic dissymmetries in order simply to exacerbate them. The global system is arranged in a way that favors super-profits for developed nations, and there are no international regulatory bodies with the will to interrupt the noncompetitive consequences of this situation.

Developing nations often have a competitive edge in readily extractable food and raw materials; they also often have large pools of cheap labor. And that is it. Their governments, one might say, have the competitive "advantage" of lacking the power or will to impose restrictions on industry, but this often simply means that these countries fail to benefit from the profit of their industries. Investments concentrate in speculative bubbles, which then burst; insufficient taxation exists to fund public works; workers remain poor and suffer from a polluted environment; and so on. Another advantage for developing countries is their enormous potential for development; if they were to be developed, the rate of profit increase, starting as it does from nothing, would clearly be incredible. But this competitive advantage remains purely abstract; it means nothing if investments are never made there.

Such development is hampered because the competitive advantages that developing nations do have are more than offset by those enjoyed by developed nations. Higher wages in the developed world mean an already existing consumer market for goods. Developing nations are strapped for cash, but developed ones have ready financing for even more capital investment. And they do not pay as much for the loans they get, since loans to them are lower risk. They have a skilled, educated workforce and the technological savvy to put them to work in industries that are highly profitable for that reason. Developed countries enjoy, in other words, the productivity gains to be had from technological innovation. While developing nations are severely restricted in what they can sell, developed nations have diversified product lines. And what they alone produce usually ensures for them very favorable terms of trade. Developing nations must import goods that require a lot of processing—higher value-added goods such as computers—and that therefore typically garner higher prices than the low value-added products of the developing world, say, food and raw materials or shoes produced with cheap labor. You have to sell, for example, an awful lot of bananas to have enough money to purchase a television set. Developed nations have politically and socially stable environments in which business can flourish. And so on.[47]

But perhaps most important in the long run, developed nations have the political and economic power to maintain these systematic advantages indefinitely, indeed to increase them exponentially. For example, we have already mentioned how developed nations extend their trade advantages through deliberate trade policy—tariffs on and domestic subsidies in the developed nations for the mostly primary goods (raw materials and food) that the undeveloped world brings to the international market. The same result often comes about from the developed world's taking advantage of the unequal exchange conse-quences of an initial situation in which developing countries are natu-rally limited in their exports to a narrow range of primary goods. For a variety of reasons—limitations on possible increased demand for food stuffs, technological innovations providing substitutes for raw material inputs in manufacturing, and so forth—primary commodity prices have the tendency to fall.[48] Underdeveloped countries, moreover, are forced, irrespective of price fluctuations in international markets for primary commodities, to glut the market in the one thing they can sell, because of their desperate need for foreign currency to pay back international loans. This depresses primary commodity prices even further and makes it even more unlikely that developing nations will be able to raise the necessary foreign capital through trade. Primary commodity prices can fall so far, indeed, that the businesses in which developing countries specialize become unprofitable. They are often indeed helped out of business by the subsidized crops of the developed world, whose imports into their own domestic markets the WTO pre-vents them from restricting. At the same time, capital flight from these same countries (because of these very economic weaknesses) prohibits diversification and their entrance into the higher value-added product lines that the developed world therefore has a de facto monopoly in.

Developed countries do their part to discourage diversification, for example, by increasing tariffs on third-world goods the more that they have been processed.[49] Developed nations in the most recent rounds of international trade negotiations have, moreover, insisted on strengthening their exclusive property rights to the technological innovations that would help developing nations diversify their industries, in exchange for loosening their own import restrictions on the sorts of goods that developing nations have to sell—agricultural products, clothing. And then they have reneged on their side of the bargain.[50]

The theological intervention here should be to join with others in pressuring international governing bodies to work to lift such conditions of ingrained systematic competitive disadvantage.[51] International trade policies must favor genuinely free and equal trade; trade concessions must be really reciprocal. Developed nations should not be allowed to nullify the competitive advantage of developing nations in raw materials and cheap labor by import restrictions, especially when export is the only way, given their limited domestic markets, that industries in the developing world can turn a profit. Where developing nations simply cannot compete effectively with developed nations in free and open international competition, they must be permitted temporarily to protect their industries from imports with the understanding that they will open their markets later.[52] Trade liberalization, in short, must be gradual, paced to the particular circumstances of the developing nations; if not, the long-term result is likely to be not increased but decreased international competition. The presently developed nations engaged in this sort of protection of their nascent industries early on; that is how they got to be developed nations. The problem is that they now want to continue that protection, even after their industries have become internationally competitive, and they want to deny to others what they had earlier. Some mechanism for debt forgiveness, moreover, has to be put in place, perhaps by way of a bankruptcy policy for nations.[53] Sources of liquidity must also be generated to enable diversification of industry in the currently underdeveloped world.[54] If market conditions do not make loans by commercial banks or foreign direct investment by transnational corporations a live possibility, then international lending bodies such as the

IMF and World Bank must be re-organized according to their original mandates to pool the surpluses of developed nations, for this very purpose.[55] TRIPS—Trade-Related Aspects of International Property Rights, which made protection of the intellectual property rights of businesses such as pharmaceutical companies in the developed world part of the mandate of the World Trade Organization in the 1990s— should be severely scaled back where these simply keep developing nations from catching up to the technological know-how of the developed world.[56] The high productivity industries of a more diversified economy would help developing nations accumulate sufficient funds for public works. Before that time, developing nations must responsibly use funds extended to them, by, say, the World Bank, for the sort of infrastructure improvements (roads, phones) and investment in people (schools, hospitals) that encourage long-term development of that sort of high-productivity economy.

The second major noncompetitive feature of capitalism becomes apparent when one considers the general snowball effect of capitalism for better or worse. Periods of both economic growth and economic decline tend, in other words, to feed on themselves in cumulative fashion. This is most obvious, and most worrisome, in the case of economic downturn and provides a warrant for the belief that capitalism is internally prone to recurrent crises, crises that can be stopped only by the external, nonmarket intervention of government.

A snowballing downturn like this of major international proportions occurred in the Great Depression. Lack of demand and loss of liquidity (that is, the tightening of credit and consequent inability of businesses to get loans) prompted cutbacks in productive investment, which led to the contraction of industries and greater unemployment. That unemployment led to further reductions in demand and to the even greater reluctance on the part of banks to supply credit for industrial expansion. Affected countries cut back on imports to spur domestic demand and in the process exported the same industrial contraction to their trading partners. These trading partners then cut back on their own imports from the originally affected economies (and still more trading partners), so as to depress the originally affected economies even further, and so on, to produce a self-perpetuating spiral of worldwide decline.

Such spirals of decline, at least in lesser degrees of severity and scope, are a constant feature of capitalism. The U.S. economy has been in one for awhile now, with stock market losses and the misallocation of funds via dot-com speculation initiating business contraction in most other sectors, leading to unemployment, which produces lack of demand, fueling further disinvestment, all in a destructive feedback loop. The Federal Reserve has been trying for the last several years, with limited success, to disrupt this destructive feedback loop through lower interest rates and the easing of credit. Those measures might jump-start productive investment and increase demand by encouraging consumers to buy on credit.

There is an obvious capitalist interest in figuring out what can be done to break these vicious spirals of decline, in which each loss feeds every other and everybody goes down together, and to replace them with the opposite sort of spiral, a virtuous spiral of mutual benefit, which the snowballing effect of capitalism also presumably allows. The opposite of the Great Depression would be an economy in which increased investment brings more jobs, those jobs lead to more demand, more demand produces greater profits, and greater profits encourage more investment, thereby bringing the cycle full circle and allowing it to feed on itself. Countries with this sort of growth engine would export it to their trading partners by the same sort of mechanism that led to the worldwide export of Depression. These countries would have, for example, an increased demand for low-cost industrial inputs bought from their less developed trading partners (say, the metals used in electronics manufacturing). And their growth engine might be stoked by increased exports of the products of such industry to them; these trading partners could now afford to buy electronic equipment with the profits made from sales of those manufacturing inputs. Increased profits from exports in the initially high-growth country would lead to increased domestic production, which would generate greater demand for imported inputs to support that production, thereby expanding the industries in those inputs of its trading partners, leading to greater employment there and greater demand for the products exported by the initially high-growth countries. And so on, thereby producing a worldwide virtuous feedback loop, from which everyone benefits.

A Mutually Beneficial Spiral?

One major point of intersection, then, between a theological economy and a capitalist one is this interest in mutually beneficial spirals. The point of intervention would be that the global economy does not presently enjoy such a spiral; even most developed nations do not experience it. A win/win spiral in the global economy is kept from emerging, in the first place, by the many measures that already developed nations take to cement into place the present win/loss structure of global capitalism that provides them with superprofits. The world seems stuck in a win/loss structure like this, in which some are enriched by beggaring others, in which some make more only as others make less. We have talked before about some of the ways this happens. Unfavorable terms of trade allow developed nations to profit as the productive capacities of the developing world are further squeezed. Cheap goods for consumers in the developed countries thereby come at the expense of continued poverty in the underdeveloped world. Capital drains into the developed countries from the developing ones that need it most, because of, for example, unfavorable schedules for foreign loan repayments. The international regulatory bodies with the power to move the world economy away from such a win/loss structure have only, as we have seen, exacerbated it by their policies.

A win/win spiral does not exist, in the second place, because the techniques for generating profit in today's world do not translate into increased demand. The preferred worldwide technique for profit generation seems to be the depression of wages and forms of corporate restructuring that produce heavy job losses. Even when corporations turn profits through productivity gains, they are not inclined to share those increased profits with their employees in the form of increased wages; the decline of organized labor in developed nations means that they feel no pressure to do so. Many developed nations are moving toward national austerity programs that depress domestic markets. A developed nation might keep the money supply tight to attract buyers of its currency. Certainly the trend in many of them, as we have discussed, is to cut back on federal infrastructure and welfare spending. As production shifts to low-wage sites in other parts of the world, no effort is made to encourage the creation of domestic markets there. Companies are happy if wages are kept low in sites of production within the developing world, despite the likely depressive effects of this on the domestic markets of those countries and even if restricted government service provision, the sort of service provision necessary to improve the business climate of these nations, proves necessary to keep wages low. In order to secure foreign debt repayment, the IMF, as we have seen, encourages every developing nation to produce for export while imposing strict restrictions on fiscal spending and the money supply, which depress their domestic markets. People in these countries cannot buy either what they sell to others or what other nations are trying to sell to them. They beggar themselves, so to speak (with a lot of encouragement from others), rather than beggar their neighbors all around by restricting imports in the manner that produced the Great Depression of the thirties. But the effect is the same: a decline in demand in most nations of the world for the goods that these nations are all trying to export.[57]

One might well, then, question the stability of the present win/loss structure of the world economy and think, with good reason, that it is tipping over into a vicious spiral of decline in which everyone loses. Fiscal and monetary austerity programs cannot be depressing domestic demand everywhere, and declining wages cannot continually be paying for profit increases, without at some point fomenting a global demand crisis and a crisis of wildly underemployed productive capacities.[58] A worry like this might indeed be what motivates the powers that be to alter the present win/loss structure of global capitalism by instituting international measures more favorable to a win/win spiral, measures like the ones mentioned above that would make the benefits of free trade more reciprocal and lift constraints on productive investment across the world.

Mitigating this worry is the belief that the current win/loss structure of global capitalism can effectively avoid crisis and head off vicious spirals of decline. Everyone does not need to win for growth to be self-sustaining in the new economy. This belief is largely premised on the idea that the new post-Fordist techniques of production, those techniques of production that make possible the globally integrated production processes of today, are not susceptible to the usual over-production/under-demand crises of earlier forms of capitalism.[59]

"Fordism" means assembly-line production and standardized mass production of a single product line. Industries organized in a Fordist way require constant growth in demand for their products in order to remain profitable; and, because of all the capital invested in machinery that can produce only one thing, they cannot respond flexibly to shifts in demand due to recession or changing consumer tastes. Post-Fordism production processes are "lean" and "flexible," by virtue of information-driven technologies, in ways that seem to obviate worries about producing more than people want to buy. For example, just-in-time production allows businesses to cut down on inventories entirely—to produce a product entirely on demand, in almost real time (by way of computer-driven communication between consumer and factory and between one division of a company and another or with its outsourcers). Flexible production—the ability of the new technologies to produce a diversified product line by switching the parts of or recalibrating the very same machines—means that companies are not hamstrung by their fixed capital investments from following new consumer trends; they are not stuck having to produce what people no longer want by the investment they have already made in machines. It also means that profit does not have to be generated by economies of scale—that is, by mass demand for a single, uniformly produced commodity. Instead, a variety of often slightly different products—think of the apparently infinite variety of Nike shoes, or special toothpaste lines for children or for professional women—can be targeted to a burgeoning number of niche markets. Helped along by heavy advertising that generates a demand for products based on the image they create rather than the needs they satisfy, a post-Fordist economy can supersaturate in this way a rather limited market. And for that reason the engines of growth can make do with a global system that includes very few winners; the engines purr along without ever greater numbers of people needing to be enabled through good-paying jobs to enter consumer markets—just so long as a few people can spend a great deal of money on the relatively small lots of different items that post-Fordist techniques of production put on these restricted consumer markets.

These post-Fordist supply-side changes in production technique are supposed to have rendered obsolete and solved the failings of the Keynesian strategies to produce virtuous economic spirals worldwide in the decades after World War II. According to those Keynesian strategies, the growing problem of limited markets and under-demand in the West could be solved by exporting the domestic virtuous spirals achieved in the West (for example, in Europe via the Marshall Plan), but at the time under threat, to undeveloped nations. The idea was to provide liquidity for investment in industries all over the world (especially to industries in countries being unfairly savaged by vicious spirals of decline) so as to generate full employment and increased aggregate demand worldwide. Because such policies were fundamentally compatible with a principle of mutual benefit, they found support in movements within third-world countries (for example, in Latin America) for import-substitutive industrialization, that is, the creation of domestic industries to produce goods previously imported from the developed West.

But in truth the strategies of international Keynesianism were never effectively implemented. The development of industries within domestic economies comparable to those of Europe or the United States was very spotty worldwide. Development was short-circuited by the almost immediate co-optation by narrower interests of the international regulatory bodies set up to institute it. Aid for economic development was extended only to those countries that were strategically important and likely allies in the Cold War fight against communism, and when the Cold War threat evaporated, so did the aid.[60] Development was short-circuited, too, by profit taking from debt peonage. Profits on risky loans at high interest rates to developing nations were much greater, at least in the short term, than profits to be had on loans for productive investment in any companies in these countries with the possibility of making money. These risky high-return loans were only encouraged, as we have seen, by IMF guarantees in effect for their pay back. International Keynesianism was sabotaged, furthermore, by the taking of technological rents; developed nations had a monopoly on the technology necessary for industrialization and therefore could charge exorbitantly for it.[61]

Both debt peonage and technological rents to developed nations were fomented by the very import-substitution strategy for growth that many developing nations especially in Latin America chose to pursue, albeit with much foreign encouragement.[62] These countries thought they could end the dependence on foreign nations that disadvantaged them, by immediately making for themselves what developed countries imported to them—such as refrigerators. They thereby squandered the few competitive advantages in, for example, cheap labor, that they had going for them. The goods they tried to make rather than import usually require for their production the very things that developing nations do not have: an educated, skilled work-force, technical know-how, and expensive machinery and the ready sources of accumulated finance capital to purchase it. Concentrating production on such goods therefore leaves developing nations at the mercy of developed nations with a competitive advantage on all those fronts.[63] These are also usually high-ticket items that only the very few already wealthy people in the limited domestic markets of developing countries can afford to buy. Lacking an adequate domestic market for what they are trying to sell, such industries are hardly likely to turn a profit.

When an adequate domestic market does not yet exist to ensure profitability, developing nations are better off initially concentrating on production for export. They should focus on industries that are labor intensive and that do not require much investment in com-plex machinery. That way they can make best use of their competi-tive advantage in cheap labor and make do with the limited finance capital they can be expected to have generated domestically. Goods like this are usually inexpensive, and people at home are not therefore priced out of the market for them. Profit can in that way be shored up by the widest possible extension of markets, to include both foreign and domestic buyers. Diversification, as we have said, is important to the strength of developing economies; they should not be stuck in labor-intensive, low-capital industries forever. But diversification into the product lines of developed nations is better brought about in the longer term using profits generated from industries that the initial competitive advantages of developing nations are able to support.[64]

We have seen, however, that there is very little in the present win/ loss organization of international capitalism to encourage such strategies for economic growth in developing nations. The post-Fordist techniques for production in the current regime of global capitalism evidently make little difference on this score. Far from being resolved by post-Fordism, the divide between winners and losers has only grown and hardened with those production techniques in place. If the win/loss character of the present post-Fordist global system is really not sustainable but prone to vicious cycles of decline like every other, we are in trouble indeed.

One can argue, then, that the resolution of overproduction/ under-demand problems is not what gives post-Fordist techniques of production their special importance. The old Fordist techniques could, as we have seen, generate their own fix: a Keynesian expansion of industrialization and domestic markets globally. Post-Fordism was not necessary, then, to resolve this problem; it just gave the developed world an easier way out than international Keynesianism, a way out that allowed the already developed world to maintain its economic dominance.

The problem that post-Fordism resolves and that Fordism cannot is a profitability problem, not an under-demand/overproduction one. In the 1970s the profit rate of industrialized nations began to decline irrespective of shifts in high and low demand worldwide. This was therefore not fundamentally a crisis of overproduction like the 1930s.[65] The usual explanation for the decline blamed organized labor; constant increases in wages paid to workers were thought responsible. But the rate of profit maintained its decline even with the success of wage cost rollbacks in the 1980s. The real culprit, apparently, is the inflexibility of fixed capital investments in Fordist production. When a firm is losing ground because of cost-cutting technical innovations made by other firms, it cannot switch easily to another line of production;

it has sunk too much money into machines, and those machines will only produce one thing. Because of all the investment in expensive equipment, a firm that is now disadvantaged by high costs will try to stick it out in the same markets and maintain its usual rate of profit by increasing market share. Lower-profit firms neither make the necessary technical innovations to catch up to their competitors' profit margins nor exit the market, as Adam Smith would predict. Instead they increase production in order to sell more and thereby foment a market glut that lowers prices and further reduces their profit. The higher-profit industries, meanwhile, are forced to put further pressure on the lower-profit ones in an effort to get them to exit the market; their higher profit margin means that they can afford to cut their prices in their own effort to increase market share. They thereby nullify their profit gains from technological innovation. The market is further glutted, pushing prices even lower. All producers match them, and the result is a decline in the rate of profit industry wide.[66]

Post-Fordist techniques of production fundamentally resolve this profitability problem by allowing firms to exit a product line immediately and enter a new one using the same equipment. These techniques simply lack, moreover, the efficiency limits of the usual Fordist production lines. With computerized coordination among the different aspects of the production process, there is no lag time between them, and the same equipment can be used almost without interruption, reprogrammed continuously to serve different segments of the same production process or to produce different inputs for a variety of product lines.

Post-Fordism does not, it is true, require the mass consumption of the same product to ensure profitability. But this does not mean that it is not dependent on growth of the total market.[67] The market for Nike shoes that glow in the dark can always remain small, but that does not mean that the market for all the slightly different sports shoes that Nike makes can remain stagnant. The fixed capital investment in post-Fordist production—say, computer equipment—is just as expensive, probably even more expensive, than under Fordism. And these investments have to be recouped quickly, since the equipment of the new technologies rapidly becomes obsolete. Companies are therefore forced to launch product lines in as many different markets as possible, indeed in every major consumer market worldwide. It is just a myth, then, that the niche marketing of post-Fordist production excludes the need for economies of scale.[68]

Aren't we in fact seeing oversupply/under-demand problems in the West and the contagion of economic decline in other areas of the world affecting our shores? How far indeed can any limited market be saturated before consumer exhaustion and backlash against the artificial elevation of false needs set in? Moreover, without any increase in mass consumption, how can social divisions and conflict not be fomented by niche marketing to the various segments of a fashion-fickle elite growing ever wealthier?[69] Aren't the inequities and exclusions of the present system breeding instability and violence all over the world—international terrorism and economic riots in countries undergoing the forced austerities of the present global system, backed by IMF restructuring policies and the threat of U.S. economic and military might?[70]

Post-Fordism, I submit, needs to be wedded to the goal of worldwide full employment and worldwide domestic market creation, or it has no long-term future. I have already suggested, in discussing government spending for welfare and infrastructure provision, that post-Fordism is compatible with Keynesian national priorities. Post-Fordist profitability funds government spending, which in turn undergirds the sort of business and employment climate that a post-Fordist economy requires. But now I am suggesting, in the interest of global economic stability, the resumption of the international Keynesian strategies that post-Fordism preempted; post-Fordism must be combined with international Keynesianism in order to avoid, at least in the long run, crippling economic crisis.

The real economy may, indeed, already be in a vicious spiral of decline. The only thing disguising that fact is the huge profit being made from the fictitious capital creation of international finance. Fictitious capital is capital that increases apart from any increase in the real production of goods and services. Additional money has to come into circulation to meet increased levels of exchange when real production goes up, but in the case of fictitious capital, money makes money without the intervention of productive investment. Loans are a very primitive form of such capital creation. And we are not just talking about interest payments here. Banks create money simply by lending their deposits.[71] Let's say someone deposits $100 in a bank. Retaining a reserve of 10 percent to pay off depositors who might want their money back, the bank can loan $90 of the original $100 to another person, who then deposits it in another bank. This new bank, in turn, can lend $81 to still another person for deposit in still another bank. And so on. At the limits of the lending process (determined by rules about what percentage of their deposits banks have to keep in reserve), the $100 has multiplied many times over.

The new global economy provides many new opportunities for fictitious capital creation.[72] The enormous amount of U.S. dollars held in foreign banks or in foreign branches of U.S. banks (so-called Petro- or Euro-dollars) is not subject to U.S. regulations on reserve deposits; without such regulations this money can be increased indefinitely as it is loaned. One can now, moreover, sell loans themselves. For example, banks can use their future earnings on mortgage loans as a kind of security to sell bonds, which investors can either keep for the interest earnings or sell in secondary markets.[73] Indeed, in today's financial markets one can turn almost any expected future earnings into instant cash.[74] The futures market, moreover, has been transformed; one is not just contracting to sell or buy some real commodity like wheat at a certain price at a certain time, but some financial product—for example, stocks in a company or a foreign currency. The buying and selling of options to either buy or sell, say, foreign currency at a certain price within a certain time ("call" options in the first case, "put" options in the second) have become important hedges against risk, since financial products change their value quite often on the open market. The value of currencies, for example, and therefore the exchange rates between them, now float on the open market. Betting on exchange rate fluctuations by buying and selling different currencies via computerized markets has become big business. An investor in Thailand, for example, who thinks the Thai currency is going to lose its value against the U.S. dollar can sell that currency for dollars and then buy it back after the decline, netting a nice profit in the Thai currency. When a lot of speculators on currency markets think the same thing, the ensuing sell-off of a currency is enough to lower its value, thereby generating profits for the speculators.[75]

The money being made from all these nonproductive monetary transactions, such as the profit from the selling of loans and currency speculation, completely dwarfs at this point the real economy of things made and consumed. One does not need to worry about the possibility of vicious cycles of decline in the real economy so long as one can still make money in these financial markets. There is, indeed, quite a lot of money to be made even when the real economy is in a tail spin. The greater the likelihood, for example, that interest rates will rise, choking off economic expansion, the more valuable the financial options that hedge against the risk of such a development. It doesn't really matter what is going on in the real economy. Expansion of the real economy is no longer necessary to increase the money for circulation in financial markets; there is more than enough to go around as it is; the financial markets themselves generate more than enough to keep these markets going indefinitely. And the money in these financial markets never has to return to the real economy. When you can sell loans themselves over and over, you don't have to worry very much about loaning for productive investment.

From a theological point of view financial markets are suspect because they are almost completely competitive. Financial markets in general are a problem on this score, but the free flow of finance capital on today's global scene only compounds the problem. Disadvantaged people—those without money—never benefit from the profit of others in unregulated capital markets. People without money are by definition not creditworthy; they either do not qualify for loans at all or must pay much higher rates of interest than those who already have money and want more. People without money are thereby further disadvantaged by the capital market. Those with money to lend to them profit from this added distress via the higher than average interest rates they pay. In the best-case scenario, people without money have to pay more for it, thereby enabling those with more money to make a better return.

The new financial markets only accentuate this competitive streak of financial exchange generally. Someone's gain is always simply someone else's loss. For example, at the first sign of weakness, I sell my currency or stock holdings faster than you do at your expense, since my selling brings down the price that you will get. The whole idea is to buy cheap and sell dear. This is true, too, for the many opportunities a worldwide financial market provides to arbitrage temporary price differences for the same sort of financial instrument in different markets. Before more people notice the opportunity and wreck the game, one buys up the cheaper instrument in one market and simultaneously, via computer technology, sells it for more on the other.[76] Free-flowing finance capital might be expected, in theory at least, to spread out to where it is needed most. For example, if a nation lacks domestic sources of funding for productive investment, it might borrow the money abroad. The reality, however, is that finance capital pools or concentrates in risk-free zones; it runs from those who need it most. Bankers do not preferentially lend to those in economic difficulty; they are much more comfortable pulling their money out of nations in that situation, which simply adds to the countries' worsening condition.[77] Ordinarily, speculation on futures in commodities helps stabilize prices.[78] For example, speculators buy surplus wheat, thereby mitigating the decline of its price, in order to stockpile it until a wheat shortage makes prices go up; they put these stockpiles on the market then, lessening the shortage and attendant price increases. Farmers are protected in times of overproduction; consumers are protected in times of underproduction. In the unregulated markets in financial instruments of today, however, every speculator rushes in at once to buy at the first sign of possible profit or to sell at the slightest hint of increased risk. In the first case, this leads to gross over-valuations, bubbles that eventually burst. In the second case, to panicked sell-offs, in which those who don't get out quickly enough suffer catastrophic losses.[79]

The unregulated international financial markets of today are indeed major forces blocking the development of a win/win spiral in the real economy. They work to hold in place, first of all, the present win/loss structure of the global real economy. When it is based on movements in the real economy, financial speculation simply does not work if there aren't winners and losers there. Thus, currencies are valued differently depending on the strengths of their respective economies, and without such differentials, trading in and out of various currencies will not garner a profit. In the second place, these markets help grow the gap between winners and losers. The more this financial speculation, based on differences in the strengths and weaknesses of the real economy of various nations, occurs, the worse the real economy differences between winners and losers become. A run on the currency of a weak economy is a financial panic that makes the economic weakness of that country far worse than it would have been otherwise. This sort of financial speculation has the capacity, in the third place, then, to be a great initiator of real economy decline spirals worldwide. For example, financial speculation seems to have been responsible in great part for the East Asian financial crisis of the 1990s.[80] The free flows of international finance only help exaggerate the cyclical ups and downs of global capitalism, turning every high and every low into a crisis. During recessions, when countries need finance capital the most to jump-start slumping businesses, finance capital flows out, thereby deepening those recessions. During boom times, finance capital rushes in from everywhere, thereby overheating the economy, putting inflationary pressures on prices, and prompting unwise over-investment— in short, setting the stage for even deeper lows to come.[81]

Today's international financial markets are simply not good for productive investment; they encourage its decline. These financial markets divert capital from productive investment by offering the possibility of greater, risk-free returns. Hot money that can be pulled out from under you in an instance cannot, moreover, satisfy the more long-term needs of businesses in the real economy. Money that flows into a country in bets on short-term exchange rate movements cannot be used to build factories or create jobs.[82] The short-term profits offered by these financial markets also force productive investments in the real economy to take a short-term view hardly compatible with productive investment. Productive investment naturally ties up money longer than financial speculation would before showing a profit, but now companies must compete for money with financial instruments that can produce huge returns in an instant by, for example, sinking large amounts of money in currency trades. One way to attract capital in these unfavorable conditions is for companies to concentrate on stock values, trying any and every technique, indeed, to increase those stock values, even at the expense of their own productive investments (for example, by way of hostile takeovers and the selling off of assets of the companies acquired). The result is the overvaluation of stock prices that eventually devastated our own stock market. Or companies simply diversify to include financial instruments and make their money that way. Money is simply diverted to nonproductive uses within a single firm. Thus, General Motors makes more money on its financial division (GMAC) than on its cars.[83] Financial markets thrive on the volatility of fluctuations in interest rates and currency values in unregulated markets, but this volatility only fosters the same short-term thinking on the part of companies. The risks and uncertainties of such a financial climate make businesses hesitate to do anything with long-term consequences.[84] Business decisions, moreover, are simply harder to make when the cost of funds for investment might increase overnight or when the prices for the various components required for production fluctuate day by day with exchange rates in the many different countries that transnational corporations now draw into the same production processes.[85] Volatility in the financial markets is not good for business.

The present organization of international financial markets also interferes with the Keynesian strategies we advocate for producing a global win/win spiral. The economies of developing countries do not grow because money that might otherwise go for investment in their industries is used instead to increase their reserves of foreign currency. These countries, for example, will add to their reserves of U.S. dollars by buying U.S. Treasury bills—by loaning their money to us, in short—in order to protect themselves against the risks from volatile capital flows that firms in their countries have incurred by taking out short-term dollar-denominated loans.[86] As we said before, the national policies that developed nations use to compete among themselves for the freewheeling finance capital of today—policies of fiscal and monetary austerity—hamper their economic growth, too, and impede increased domestic demand. High interest rates, for example, may attract buyers of your currency, but they depress capital investment in productive industries and with it the jobs such capital investment is likely to create. Finally, in the effort to compete for money with the risk-hedged financial markets that offer short-term profits and in order to keep their own stock valuations as high as possible, companies in the developed world feel pressure to appear as profitable as possible, at the expense of their workers. Even though productivity gains enable increased profits without any of this being necessary, companies in the new post-Fordist economy still slash wages and benefits and let workers go in order to cut every possible expense from their books. Increased aggregate demand for their products is necessary for the profits of high-productivity industries to keep increasing without job and wage cuts—especially as these technological innovations spread across the board.[87] But such increased aggregate demand is highly unlikely where high-productivity industries take the course of downsizing right from the start, as if their very profitability depended on it.

The real economy across the globe will continue to decline, and those with the power to do anything about it will raise nary a whimper, unless measures are taken to discourage financial speculation and make productive investments more attractive. The return to something like pre-70s fixed international exchange rates would, for example, do away with speculation in currency markets. Keeping worldwide interest rates low or imposing taxes on financial trades (for example, taxes on cross-border currency exchanges or taxes on the buying and selling of stocks) might help equalize the profits with productive investment. Taxes like those would also dampen the volatility of financial markets and help lessen their short-term character. One would have to hold a currency or stock longer in order to recover the cost of the tax on the initial trade.[88] Opportunities for arbitrage could also be limited by harmonizing market regulations in the different markets for financial products; for example, identical margins could be required in stock, futures, and option markets. One could also bring regulations in markets for the same financial products across the world into line with one another; taxes on stock trades, for example, would in that case be the same in Japan as they are in Germany.[89]

Developing nations must be able to protect themselves against speculative runs on their currency, by, for example, putting limits on the freedom with which their currency can be exchanged for others. They must also be able to direct the flow of financing within their countries so that it goes where it is most needed. Rather than fueling, say, real estate speculation, money should be channeled to those industries most important for their national development and into investments that help overcome their competitive disadvantages on the world stage—into education, infrastructure projects, and research and development for new industries.[90] In developing countries, in short, any lifting of controls on finance capital has to be gradual.[91] Financial markets need, moreover, to be re-regulated, their free flows curtailed, by way of some of the measures previously mentioned, so that developed nations are not forced to set national priorities that favor international finance over economic growth and full employment. The dominance of finance over the needs of the real economy in the developed world should not be permitted to continue.

International bodies like the IMF and World Bank with the power to influence worldwide investment patterns should, furthermore, take steps to set up international funding sources that would do for the global economy what a federal bank ordinarily does for a national economy.[92] In the United States, for example, the job of the Federal Reserve is to set up a monetary policy that dampens the natural tendency of money to pile in when the going is good and flee when times get difficult. Moving in the opposite direction of these natural inclinations of finance capital, the Fed tightens the supply of money when the economy is booming and eases credit in times of a downturn. Moreover, federal regulations on U.S. banks keep money from running, as it naturally will, to areas of lowest risk, and shift it, by way of laws like the Community Reinvestment Act, to where it is needed most.[93] Banks are required by such laws to lend at good terms to low-income areas that would otherwise be underserved by credit agencies. International loans for development made, for example, by the World Bank should follow much the same policies: developed countries awash in finance capital should pay at least market rates, while developing countries in the greatest need of capital should have their rates subsidized. Rather than paying more interest, as a free financial market would dictate, they should pay less or none at all.[94] The IMF, meanwhile, should return to its original mandate and free up money for countries in economic crisis rather than putting the screws to them.[95] On the international as well as the national level, then, the essentially competitive character of financial markets should be dampened by counter-measures like these.

Non-Marketable Goods and Noncompetitive Possession and Use

Finally, let's raise the question of possible forms of mutual benefit that exceed the abilities of capital markets to provide. Here would be a point of theological intervention, following the principle of noncompetitiveness, that leads beyond the market. Vicious spirals of decline can be stopped and virtuous spirals of mutual advance initiated only by way of nonmarket mechanisms—that is, through the deliberate intervention of national and, now, given the present economy of global interdependencies, international regulatory bodies. But these are merely nonmarket interruptions to an overall market framework. The means to the mutual benefit of a win/win scenario might not be reducible to market forces, but the ultimate goal still is. Isn't it also possible that there are simply states or forms of mutual good beyond those achievable by market forces?

Economists usually express the optimal scenario of mutual benefit that can be achieved under market conditions as the Pareto optimum (after Vilfredo Pareto).[96] The Pareto optimum is that point at which no one can be made better off without someone else being made worse off. Measures that benefit only some people are fine, so long as others get some benefit too or are simply not harmed in the process. Every measure like this should, indeed, be taken until one runs out of options and reaches the point where steps taken to benefit some would be offset by harms to others. That point is the Pareto optimum.

A society where gaps in incomes produced by the market are closed would be an example of a state of mutual benefit that exceeds what the Pareto optimum calls for. The Pareto optimum is compatible with all kinds of differences in income distribution, even quite extreme ones.

The incomes of some can increase much faster than those of others or increase while those of others remain flat, thereby enlarging the gap between those in high- and low-income brackets. None of that is worrisome from the standpoint of the Pareto optimum, so long as lower-income folks are not made that much worse off in the process. Worrisome, instead, are efforts to close the income gap by income redistribution. Those efforts always seem in and of themselves to violate the Pareto optimum. Income redistribution, say, by way of the tax system, essentially just means taking away from those better off for the benefit of those less fortunate.

But from the point of view of a theological principle of mutual benefit, income differentials of any significance are not the ideal: everyone has a right to the same benefit. Nor are those differentials the ideal even from a simply capitalist point of view. At sufficiently extreme levels they produce social instability, and that is bad for business. And as we have mentioned so many times before, more people with more money to spend helps stoke the engines of capitalism.

The ultimate needs of the market do not seem then in this case to jive very well with what the Pareto optimum suggests is the most one can hope for under market conditions. This surprising disjunction between the two might, indeed, give one a reason to question whether income redistribution really violates the Pareto optimum. Perhaps the idea that it does exaggerates, for example, the extent to which a progressive income tax harms a very rich person for the benefit of others. What dent does even a very high tax rate really make in the lifestyle of a person with a billion dollars? If the money from these taxes goes to fill the pockets of very poor people, won't the benefits to them outweigh any cost borne by the rich? The economic principles of theological economy suggest, moreover, that possible benefits to the wealthy from income redistribution are being underestimated. The usual understanding of the Pareto optimum does not factor in the interest one might have in another's benefit, the way what others have might be one's own, through one's identification with them and one's ability to draw on what they have for one's own good. It also ignores the way that people might have an individual interest in what benefits the community or society as a whole. What benefits a person is, in short, too narrowly defined in individualistic terms. Those who give up a portion of their income to elevate the real incomes of the less fortunate will be paid back out of the economic benefits to everyone from a more uniformly well-off populace.

However the Pareto optimum is understood and applied, it is fairly uncontroversial from both a theological and an economic point of view to believe that markets do not do anywhere near as good a job with income distribution as they do with resource allocation.[97] Almost every modern economy, consequently, includes nonmarket mechanisms for income redistribution, such as some form of progressive income tax. More equalized income distribution might very well be, then, an example of a scenario of mutual benefit beyond anything achievable through market forces.

Surprisingly enough, on the score of resource allocation, too, there are situations in which markets are inefficient and fail to reach even the Pareto optimum. These are situations in which costs and benefits are not directly monetizable, that is, not fully reflected in the prices charged for goods, and consequently fall outside the bounds of market transactions. Economists call eventualities like these, appropriately enough, externalities.[98] At its most general, an externality simply means that people who have not been a party to it feel the effects for better or worse of a market transaction. Externalities of both kinds—good and bad—are only likely to become more common in a world of globalized interdependencies, where, for example, a capital flight panic in China has the potential to bring down the stock market in New York.

In the case where a benefit is not monetized, people benefit others without being compensated. This holds for so-called public goods, which are those that pricing mechanisms cannot exclude anyone from enjoying once they have been produced. A lighthouse is an example; one cannot limit the boats that enjoy its benefits to those willing to pay for the help they receive from it in avoiding dangerous shoals. Since one cannot charge for their use, the production of public goods is never adequately compensated through the usual market mechanisms. You can never recover the costs of production because you cannot make people pay for the use of what you have produced. These goods are therefore never produced in sufficient quantities via market mechanisms, and that means the Pareto optimum of social benefit is never reached in their case. Sailors would be better off with a lighthouse, but the market does not have the means to supply one.

Indeed, it is hard to generate sufficient funds for the production of public goods using even nonmarket mechanisms.[99] One might try, for example, to solicit the requisite funds by taking up a collection from all those who would benefit from a public good's production. Despite the fact that they recognize they would benefit from its production, not many people are likely to contribute to such a fund voluntarily, for a variety of reasons. First of all, there is the so-called free-rider problem. Every one will benefit from the production of a public good whether they have paid for its production or not, and therefore none of them has an interest in expending the money to create it: they would rather have other people pay and enjoy the benefits for free. Second, because one's own contribution is negligible relative to the total amount required, there is no point in contributing if others won't, and there is no guarantee they will when contributions are voluntary. If I cannot count on the fact that others will contribute too, I am likely to lose the money I contribute without gaining any benefit at all. Third, sufficient funds might be assured if a very few people contributed a very great deal, but one would be banking in that case on the rare occurrence of self-sacrificial altruism: these individuals would always be paying out quite a bit more than they would ever get back from the production of a public good, since the benefit to any one individual from a public good is usually not very much. The common solution to such problems is for government to raise the funds, by making it a law that everyone contribute a small amount commensurate with the benefits they will receive as individuals from the production of a public good.[100]

In the case where a cost is not monetized, it does not form part of a company's costs of production that have to be recouped by being incorporated into the selling price of its products. A company does not have to pay for the resources it uses up in production or for the harms the production process generates if there are no price tags attached to those things. Such costs, as a result, neither cut into the profit of the seller nor have to be borne by the buyer via higher prices. These costs are instead fobbed onto those outside the market transaction. Environmental costs—natural resource depletion and pollution—are costs like this. Those doing the damage or encouraging the damage by buying the products do not have to pay for it, and therefore the market does nothing to discourage forms of production with these environmental costs. The market itself for such products is, indeed, distorted, since the selling price does not fully incorporate, as it should, all costs of production. The demand for such products is inflated beyond what the market would bear if prices accurately reflected actual costs. Such industries also appear more cost-effective, more efficient and profitable, than they actually are; they therefore attract more capital investment than is warranted. If the result in the case of unmonetized benefits of production was a less than optimal underproduction of public goods, here in the case of unmonetized costs the result is therefore harmful overproduction. Government has the right, once again, to step in, this time in order to put restraints on the expansion of such industries.[101]

Such negative externalities—externalities that do harm to parties outside the market transaction—violate one of the main theological principles under the rubric of noncompetitiveness: one shall not benefit at another's expense. The theological intervention here would then be to encourage government regulation to flush them out of the system. Rather than fob them onto others, the producers and consumers of, say, resource depleting and polluting goods must be made to bear the costs themselves or made to compensate others for harms done to them. Government could do that by way of either taxes or quotas.[102] A tax, for example, could be levied on heavy resource depleting or polluting industries. This would have a direct effect on the level of production and consumption in such industries by raising the cost of production and therefore the price of the product. The tax revenues could also be used for environmental clean up or to subsidize energy-efficient and pollution-decreasing technologies. If this sort of tax would create large-scale economic hardship, for example, by making heating oil too expensive for most people to purchase, a much smaller, universally borne income tax earmarked for environmental programs might present an alternative. Governments could also produce much the same effect through quotas on resource depletion and pollution emissions. Quotas on resource depletion create a kind of artificial scarcity in natural resources that increases their market value and with it the likelihood that companies will have to pay for them.[103] Or pollution permits setting limits on acceptable emission levels could be issued to companies. These might be traded on the open market, thereby giving a competitive edge to low-polluting industries: they could sell their permits to higher-polluting ones, thereby lowering their costs and increasing those of their competitors.

Pollution and resource depletion are international externality problems requiring international solutions. Here again international regulatory bodies would have to get into the act, with the authority, for example, to collect tax revenues on polluting industries worldwide. In a world of rampant negative externalities, countries will always be tempted to gain competitive advantage by lowering their environmental standards. This must be stopped by setting international environmental minimums.[104] If a theological principle of least sacrifice is followed, those who pay on the international scene would be the ones who could most afford to, those for whom such payment would cause minimal hardship. Developed nations, for example, might better afford heavy taxes on energy-intensive industries, since they have the financing and technical know-how to improve industrial energy efficiency, and a sufficiently diversified economy to shift economic growth to other economic sectors.[105] Care should also be taken to prevent international environmental regulations from stifling economic growth in developing nations. The good of economic growth in countries where billions live in poverty might more than offset short-term environmental harms.[106] The poverty inflicted there by a no-growth environmental policy can be just as environmentally devastating, moreover, as a policy promoting energy-depleting and polluting growth. Just because they are short on money, poor people are often forced, for example, to farm in an unsustainable way, using more and more land and shorter and shorter crop rotation cycles.[107] If no- or low-growth environmental strategies do not make sense for developing nations, attention should be focused, instead, on the *sort* of growth that international regulations encourage.[108] Funds for international development could, for example, foster the transfer of know-how and equipment for new energy-saving technologies from developed to developing nations.

The theological intervention in the case of positive externalities—externalities where benefits to others are not monetized—is more complicated, especially insofar as these externalities involve public goods. On the face of it, we simply have here another violation of a sub-principle under the more general theological principle of noncompetitiveness: thou shalt not benefit others at one's own expense. And that would mean that here too the theological recommendation would be to rid the market of them. Closer inspection suggests, however, that public goods are the ideal in that they conform to the theological principles of noncompetitive possession and use. Public goods prove a real-life instantiation of such principles. The outstanding feature of public goods is that everyone can enjoy the whole of them at the same time with the complete absence of rivalry (think of the previous example of a lighthouse). A public good exists, an economist would say, in indivisible joint supply: We all enjoy the whole of it—that is the meaning of "indivisibility" here—and we all manage to benefit at the same time, without any one person's enjoyment taking away from anyone else's—that is the meaning of "joint." Everyone is able to use a public good in its entirety, it seems, without using it up. Public goods are also nonappropriable:[109] everyone benefits from a public good without having to appropriate it for themselves, without having to make it their individual private property. Public goods are neither mine nor yours and are enjoyed by all nonetheless, in the absence of any private property rights. The fact that they do not have to be privately appropriated in order to be enjoyed is just what explains in great part the difficulties in getting people to pay for using them.

Public goods show the general viability of what the theological principles of noncompetitive possession and use call for. Countering the suspicion we have had about this along the way, goods conforming to such principles are not, for example, limited to mental goods, that is, intellectual property. The public goods for which governments provide funding—lighthouses, roads, national defense systems, public squares, vaccination programs—are quite a diverse lot. Many public goods—like our favorite example of a lighthouse—are quite physical. Public goods have, indeed, no necessary connection with mental goods. A piece of knowledge can be shared as a whole by all at the very same time without rivalry, but it is also quite possible to turn knowledge into private property, for example, by enforcing copyright laws.

Public goods also make clear how theological principles of noncompetition do not require for their viability the unlikely eventuality of superabundance in a world of scarcity. Goods in superabundant supply have only a superficial similarity with public goods.[110] Where a good, such as water, exists in vast quantities, it is true that one person's partaking of it will not stand in the way of any other person's doing so. This presents only a superficial similarity with the case of a public good, however, since the water I drink is privately appropriated and is therefore no longer available for your use. We do not drink the same gulp of water; the gulp I drink is no longer available to you. Eventual scarcity problems affecting natural resources prove this point of difference. Public goods do not become scarce as more and more people use them the way natural resources do, because they are not used up. A public good, moreover, does not have to exist in vast quantities. To serve all the boats floating by, a million lighthouses are not required; one will do. Total demand is often satisfied in the case of a public good through the production of a single unit, since everyone is able to make use of the very same thing.

Finally, the real-world example of public goods helps explain how it is possible for enjoyment to be noncompetitive where property is held in common, as our theological principles recommend. In the case of public goods, everyone enjoys the very same good but consumption by one person does not diminish the amount of that good available to others. It makes perfect sense then to believe, in accord with our theological principle of noncompetitiveness, that one need not benefit at the expense of others and that they need not benefit at yours. This is not a utopian hope. For the same reason, the total property held in common also need not diminish in amount as everyone draws upon it for their own good. Holding property in common, so that it is no more mine than yours and so that we both are able to draw upon it for our benefit, need not mean that the amount of property owned in common is progressively depleted. Scarcity problems simply do not arise here to promote competition.

In the case of externalities causing harm to others, the usual solution, with which a theological economy would concur, is for governments to intervene to establish an efficient market in the products at issue. Governments work to establish an efficient market by finding ways to monetize costs that producers and consumers of these products would otherwise not have to pay for. As we have seen, governments, for example, impose taxes on production or consumption so that costs are internalized in the prices to be paid. One could try to solve the under-provision problems of public goods in the same way—by making people pay for access to them. The very nature of public goods often makes this, however, too costly or not very feasible: public goods are just ones that when available to one person become automatically available to everybody else.[111] Some public goods, though, are fairly easy to restrict to those paying a fee: think of tolls on a bridge. New technologies, moreover, increase the possibilities for monetizing access to public goods. Indeed, new technologies allow for the commodification of all kinds of previously free things: you can now be charged for incoming calls to your phone, even for calls that you didn't answer.[112] It might then become increasingly practical and economically feasible to charge for access to public goods. For example, every boat that comes into range of a lighthouse might now be charged using some sort of electronic pass system like that employed on some highways.

Unlike the case of negative externalities, pricing mechanisms are not sufficient, however, to produce an efficient market in public goods.[113] Public goods retain a number of odd features that disrupt market efficiency, even when people are made to pay for them. For example, these goods are unusual in that no increased costs accrue as more people enjoy them. The costs of producing and maintaining a lighthouse are the same, for example, whether one boat or two million benefit from the light it provides. A major reason for this lack of increased costs is the simple fact that the company producing them does not have to make any more of them to meet increased demand; production need not increase as the number of people enjoying these goods goes up. Because costs do not increase as these goods are extended to more people, the market dictates that the fee for using them should be zero. If one doesn't charge for access, however, the typically enormous costs of production are never recovered. If, in order to deal with this difficulty, one charges to recover costs, the price will always be more than the market will bear. People should not be paying anything, after all, and therefore fewer people will use the public good than would if the price accurately reflected the market. The Pareto optimum for that reason is never achieved, even with the introduction of pricing mechanisms. Charging for use interferes, moreover, with the usual market mechanism signaling that production be stopped; one never reaches, in other words, that point where profits from making one more item would be matched by the costs of producing it. Since there are no costs from extending access to more people, profits only go up as more people pay the charges. Production of a public good for which people are charged is therefore more profitable than it should be according to principles of market efficiency.

Making people pay for access, in short, is itself a violation of what market principles suggest in the case of public goods: you are passing on costs to people that they haven't made you incur; no costs should mean free access. And this is indeed what the theological principle of unconditional giving itself would suggest. Making payment a condition for receiving what one would otherwise get for free is a particularly egregious violation of that principle. The better course is to find ways of funding their production that do not interfere with their free use by everyone.[114] Small, universally borne taxes to generate public subsidies for their production would, for example, solve the underproduction problem of public goods in that sort of way. These taxes would replace the need to restrict access to those who pay a fee for it. Private firms producing public goods might be compensated from the government treasury using such tax revenues. If these goods are genuinely public, there should be a massive universal benefit accruing from their production; costs of production could therefore be paid from tax revenues on those future benefits. Costs would thereby be paid at no one's real expense, in a way that accords, too, with a theological principle of least sacrifice.

Making people pay for access to public goods privatizes them and therefore destroys their character as public goods. Some people are now excluded from using them by way of the introduction of a pricing mechanism. These goods lose, in other words, their nonexclusive character. And their benefits are no longer distributed universally so as to obviate any possibility of rivalry. They are no longer marked by joint supply. This privatizing of public goods is only happening more and more today as the functions of government on the global scene are hollowed out and the contributions of government to welfare provision decline.

But according to theological principles of economy, public goods are the ideal, and therefore, rather than try to rid the world of them, we should be working to multiply them. Instead of making every public good a private one by charging people for it, theological principles suggest one should be turning everything for which one could be charged into a good freely available on noncompetitive terms. It is not so much the intrinsic features of a thing that determines whether it is a public good but public policy.[115] Many more things can therefore be turned into public goods than one might first expect.

Public goods are turned into private ones by laws that create, for example, patents and copyright protections. New technologies may make charging for all sorts of things a possibility, but this will not become a reality apart from the decision of legislators and the courts. Turning a public good into a private one also usually involves the construction of barriers and police enforcement of restrictions on access. What a society puts in place, a society can also remove.

Exclusion and nonexclusion, unconditional rights of access or payment for the privilege, are all evidently matters for political decision. Joint supply might seem an intrinsic feature of public goods beyond the reach of anything public policy might influence. Superabundance, for example, is often assumed to be such a necessary prerequisite, but we dismissed its importance earlier for joint supply: the fact that everyone benefits from a public good has nothing to do with that good's being plentiful.

Indeed, depending on the range from which one views them, in either tight close-up or more expansively at further remove, all market transactions of a private sort have the capacity to take on the character of joint supply that marks public goods.[116] For example, my ability to purchase food is not a public good in joint supply in that the food I consume leaves just that much less for everybody else. But the fact of everyone's being able to purchase enough food to eat is a public good of that sort. Everyone benefits economically from living in such a society. And my enjoyment of the good of that society doesn't come at the expense of your enjoyment: we both, for example, eat our fill. The same with employment: my getting the job means you don't. But full employment is a public good in that, as I have said so many times in this chapter, everyone benefits economically from it. My being employed in that case does not come at your expense.

In short, private goods at a society-wide level turn into public ones. At that level, they amount, indeed, to the very sorts of goods that I have been trying to make the center of the global agenda in this chapter: growth buttressed by full employment at high wages, by poverty reduction, and by increasing worldwide demand. Like public goods generally, these goods have provision problems that are best resolved through collective government initiatives, this time at an international level.[117] We have talked throughout this chapter about the sort of steps that would be necessary.

The Will for Change

Theological principles draw attention to this public good character of all private goods and remind us that, while market forces cannot efficiently supply them, such goods are ours for the taking if only we had the communal will to implement them. *Will* is the operative word here. At the end of our long ruminations on theology and economy, we now have a sense of the whole new shape that global economy would take when pushed and pulled by forces of theological economy. We also know the sort of things that would have to happen in order for a new global economy like that to become a reality. But how might the will for such changes be generated? What might get the world to change?

As in every previous alteration of capitalism by social forces, those disadvantaged by the current system are the ones most motivated to fight for change. These people, however, are unlikely for the same reason to be in positions of power. What they are therefore immediately agitating for is greater influence over the course of their lives. That might mean, on the present scene, greater representation within the international governing bodies with the power to alter the current organization of global capitalism. As it stands, for example, the greater your economic power the more votes you have in the IMF, and the country with the greatest economic power, the United States, enjoys sole veto rights.[118] International institutions of governance will have to be made more accountable to those harmed by the present system, if such institutions are ever to take the lead in changing the present workings of the global system.

Those disadvantaged by the present system are scattered across the globe, but they can be mobilized to put joint pressure on such international organizations through much the same mechanisms that help scatter them—for example, the new computer technologies that allow for the networking of diverse organizations via the internet. New forms of mobilization will in that way come to match the new forms of the problem, international exploitation of possibilities for superprofits, for example, confronting international coordination of nongovernmental organizations (NGOs) working to change the same systemic economic inequities. In the same way that it makes sense to organize the workers on the same shop floor—despite all the racial and ethnic differences that divide them and despite company efforts to get them to see one another as competitors—it now makes sense for workers in one country to align their interests with those in another: after all, they are both employed, either directly or indirectly, by the same transnational corporations.[119]

People disadvantaged by the present system are likely to be joined in their efforts to change things by at least a few people benefiting from the system who nonetheless find it appalling on moral and religious grounds. This book tries to provide such grounds for Christians, especially in the United States, advantaged beyond all decent proportions by the present system. The more economic benefits we enjoy, the more power we are likely to have to change things. We should use that power—say, the power of our vote in the most economically dominant nation on earth—to put pressure on the U.S. government to change its policies for international trade and financing agreements that only further disadvantage the already disadvantaged around the globe.

Such broad-based agitation might make it worth the while of the powers that be to change things, especially when they know that the changes called for will only benefit them, too, in the long run. Expressions of global disgruntlement by a united coalition of the many harmed and the morally outraged few might make it cost-effective, so to speak, for those in control to modify their support of the present system, since it is only in their own long-term interest to do so. History demonstrates that those hurt by capitalism succeed in changing the system only where that change serves the general interest—the interests, in short, of capitalists too.[120] Holding out the theological vision of a universally inclusive community of mutual benefit as our moral compass, this book has tried to show how the goal we seek is of that sort—a global economy re-organized to avoid crisis by advantaging everyone.

NOTES

1. An Economy of Grace?

1. Kathryn Tanner, *Theories of Culture: A New Agenda for Theology*, Guides to Theological Inquiry (Minneapolis: Fortress Press, 1997), chapter 5.

2. Political and liberation theologies often raise the question of how central Christian beliefs are bound up with everyday judgments of a political and economic sort. For my own analysis of the matter, see Kathryn Tanner, *The Politics of God: Christian Theologies and Social Justice* (Minneapolis: Fortress Press, 1992), especially chapter 1.

3. Max Weber, *The Protestant Ethic and the Spirit of Capitalism*, trans. Talcott Parsons (New York: Scribners, 1958).

4. For the general understanding of signs as "substitutes" or "stand-ins" for what they signify, see Jean-Joseph Goux, *Symbolic Economies,* trans. Jennifer Curtiss Gage (Ithaca, N.Y.; Cornell University Press, 1990), 1–3.

5. H. Richard Niebuhr, *The Social Sources of Denominationalism* (New York: Meridian, 1959).

6. The term "iron cage" is Max Weber's. See *Protestant Ethic*, 181.

7. See Ferdinand de Saussure, *Course in General Linguistics,* trans. Wade Baskin (New York: Philosophical Library, 1959). Claude Levi-Strauss turned structuralism into a comparative method. See, for example, his *Structural Anthropology,* trans. C. Jacobson and B. Schoepf (New York: Basic, 1973).

8. See Max Weber, *The Sociology of Religion*, trans. Ephraim Fischoff (Boston: Beacon, 1963).

9. For the basics of Bourdieu's account of a "general science of economy," see, among other works, Pierre Bourdieu, *Outline of a Theory of Practice*, trans. Richard Nice (Cambridge: Cambridge University Press, 1977), 171–99; *Distinction: A Social Critique of the Judgment of Taste*, trans. Richard Nice (Cambridge, Mass.: Harvard University Press, 1984); *In Other Words: Essays towards a Reflexive Sociology*, trans. Matthew Adamson (Stanford, Calif.: Stanford University Press, 1990); and *The Field of Cultural Production: Essays on Art and Literature* (New York: Columbia University Press, 1993).

10. Goux, *Symbolic Economies.*

11. See Pierre Bourdieu, *Pascalian Meditations,* trans. Richard Nice (Stanford, Calif.: Stanford University Press, 2000), 172–75; and *Distinction,* 232–34, 468–70.

12. See, for example, Bourdieu, *Outline,* 177–78, 183; and *In Other Words,* 92–93, 106–15, 140–44.

13. See Pierre Bourdieu, *Acts of Resistance: Against the Tyranny of the Market,* trans. Richard Nice (New York: Free Press, 1999), 81–87.

14. Bourdieu, *Outline,* 177–78, 183.

15. See, for example, the very revealing *Distinction,* 228.

16. Bourdieu, *In Other Words,* 143–44.

17. See Max Weber, "The Social Psychology of the World Religions," in *From Max Weber: Essays in Sociology,* trans. and ed. H. H. Gerth and C. Wright Mills (New York: Oxford University Press, 1946), 287–88.

18. See Friedrich Schleiermacher, *On Religion,* trans. John Oman (New York: Harper and Row, 1958), Fourth Speech.

19. Donald G. Mathews, *Religion in the Old South,* Chicago History of American Religion (Chicago: University of Chicago Press, 1977), 219.

20. Niebuhr, *Social Sources* , 28.

21. *Phaedrus,* 248 a–b; 252c–253c, trans. R. Hackforth, in *The Collected Dialogues of Plato,* ed. Edith Hamilton and Huntington Cairns (Princeton, N.J.: Princeton University Press, 1963).

22. 29e, trans. Benjamin Jowett, in the *Collected Dialogues of Plato.*

23. Martin Luther, *Luthers Werke: Kritische Gesamtausgabe,* 10:1.1, translation in Anders Nygren, *Agape and Eros* (Chicago: University of Chicago Press, 1982), 735 n. 1.

24. *Purgatorio,* Canto 15, lines 67–75, trans. John Ciardi (New York: Mentor, 1957).

25. Niebuhr, *Social Sources,* 267.

2. Imagining Alternatives to the Present Economic System

1. For examples of the way anthropology and history fund socio-cultural criticism—examples that will figure in my own argument to come—see Marshall Sahlins, *Stone Age Economics* (Chicago: Aldine/Atherton, 1972); and James Tully, *A Discourse on Property: John Locke and His Adversaries* (Cambridge: Cambridge University Press, 1980), x; and *An Approach to Political Philosophy: Locke in Contexts* (Cambridge: Cambridge University Press, 1993), 1, 127: "I have sought to develop an approach to political philosophy that throws light on the problems of the present age through contextual studies of the history of modern political thought" (1).

2. For more on the basics of a capitalist understanding of property from a historical perspective, see C. B. Macpherson, "Human Rights as Property Rights," *Dissent* (winter 1997): 72–77.

3. For an astute analysis and criticism of this view, see Simon Clarke, *Marx, Marginalism, and Modern Sociology: From Adam Smith to Max Weber* (London: MacMillan, 1982).

4. See the very moving stories in David K. Shipler, *The Working Poor: Invisible in America* (New York: Knopf, 2004).

5. For this interpretation of Locke, see Tully, *An Approach to Political Philosophy*; and Ruth W. Grant, *John Locke's Liberalism* (Chicago: University of Chicago Press, 1987).

6. For an expanded treatment of the ideas in this paragraph, see C. B. Macpherson, "The Meaning of Property," in *Property: Mainstream and Critical Positions*, ed. C. B. Macpherson (Toronto: University of Toronto Press, 1978), 7.

7. See Carole Pateman, *The Sexual Contract* (Stanford, Calif.: Stanford University Press, 1988), 150–51.

8. This ambiguity lies behind the different ways Locke is read by Tully in his *An Approach to Political Philosophy*, and by C. B. Macpherson, *The Political Theory of Possessive Individualism: Hobbes to Locke* (Oxford: Clarendon, 1962).

9. See Tully, *An Approach to Political Philosophy*, 102–17, esp. 105–6, 111–12, 114–16.

10. Macpherson, *Political Theory*, 202.

11. See Jean Baudrillard, *The Mirror of Production*, trans. Mark Poster (St. Louis: Telos, 1975), for a systematic attack on the centrality in economic thinking of the concept of labor. The primary opponent is Marxism.

12. See B. A. Gerrish, *Grace and Gratitude: The Eucharistic Theology of John Calvin* (Minneapolis: Fortress Press, 1993).

13. John Calvin, *Institutes of the Christian Religion*, ed. John T. McNeill, trans. Ford Lewis Battles, vol. 1 (Philadelphia: Westminster, 1960 [1559]), 822, 837.

14. Ibid., 790.

15. Ibid., 791.

16. Ibid., 840.

17. Ibid., 723, 695, 720.

18. Ibid., 791, 790.

19. Ibid., 801–2, 796.

20. Ibid., 805.

21. See John Milbank, "Can a Gift Be Given?" *Modern Theology* 11/1 (January 1995): 119–61; Catherine Pickstock, *After Writing: On the Liturgical Consummation of Philosophy*, Challenges in Contemporary Theology (Oxford: Blackwell, 1998); Stephen H. Webb, *The Gifting God: A Trinitarian Ethics of Excess* (Oxford: Oxford University Press, 1996); and M. Douglas Meeks, *God the Economist: The Doctrine of God and Political Economy* (Minneapolis: Fortress Press, 1989). The exact natures of the respective appeals by these theologians to noncommodity gift exchange are too complicated to go into here. These appeals are, for example, far from uncritical. But using Milbank as our touchstone here, one can nevertheless say that the theological account

of grace is often proposed simply as a modified version of these exchanges. Milbank talks of them as a kind of "advent" of his own Christian view of gift giving; he is attempting to purify their agonistic and closed character, while maintaining the priority on reciprocal relations and on nonrepetitive creative response that defines them.

22. C. A. Gregory, *Gifts and Commodities* (London: Academic, 1982), 12.

23. See, for example, Arjun Appadurai, "Introduction: Commodities and the Politics of Value," in *The Social Life of Things*, ed. Arjun Appadurai (Cambridge: Cambridge University Press, 1986), 11–16.

24. See Jean-Joseph Goux, "General Economics and Postmodern Capitalism," *Yale French Studies* 78 (1990): 206–24.

25. Marcel Mauss, *The Gift: The Form and Reason for Exchange in Archaic Societies*, trans. W. D. Halls (New York: Norton, 1990), 74.

26. See Lewis Hyde, *The Gift: Imagination and the Erotic Life of Property* (New York: Vintage, 1979), 86, 88, 115, 134–36.

27. Pierre Bourdieu, *Outline of a Theory of Practice* (Cambridge: Cambridge University Press, 1977), is a famous proponent of this idea. This implicitly contractual character does not mean that gift exchanges are not genuinely such (that would assume an abstract or merely different account of gift's defining features); it just means that occlusion of obligation (among other things) defines this sort of giving.

28. See Maurice Godelier, *The Enigma of the Gift*, trans. Nora Scott (Chicago: University of Chicago Press, 1999).

29. See Hyde, *The Gift*, 101–2. This is not to say that women in gift economies have no power themselves as givers; cf. Annette Weiner, *Women of Value, Men of Renown: New Perspectives in Trobriand Exchange* (Austin: University of Texas Press, 1976).

30. For more on modern philanthropy, see Ilana Silber, "Modern Philanthropy," in *Marcel Mauss: A Centenary Tribute*, ed. Wendy James and N. J. Allen, Methodology and History in Anthropology 1 (New York: Berghahn, 1998).

31. See Pierre Bourdieu, *Pascalian Meditations*, trans. Richard Nice (Stanford, Calif.: Stanford University Press, 2000), 193, 198; and Jean-Luc Marion, *Prolegomena to Charity*, trans. Stephen E. Lewis (New York: Fordham University Press, 2002), 1–30.

32. See David Cheal, *The Gift Economy* (London: Routledge, 1988).

33. See Pierre Bourdieu, *The Field of Cultural Production: Essays on Art and Literature* (new York: Columbia University Press, 1993), 112–41; Jonathan Parry, "The Gift, the Indian Gift and the 'Indian Gift,'" *Man* (New Series) 21/3 (September 1986): 453–73; and Alan Silver, "Friendship in Commercial Society," *The American Journal of Sociology* 95/6 (May 1990): 1474–1504.

34. Parry, "The Gift, the Indian Gift," 458.

35. Ibid., 466.

36. See Jean-Luc Marion, *Being Given: Toward a Phenomenology of Givenness*, trans. Jeffrey L. Kosky, Cultural Memory in the Present (Stanford, Calif.: Stanford University Press, 2002).

37. Cheal, *Gift Economy*, 5.

38. For a summary of the literature on this point, see James G. Carrier, *Gifts and Commodities: Exchange and Western Capitalism since 1700*, Material Cultures (London: Routledge, 1995), 199–200.

39. See Jacques Derrida, *Given Time: I. Counterfeit Money*, trans. Peggy Kamuf (Chicago: University of Chicago Press, 1992), for the most famous hyperbolic effort to purify the category of gift along the following lines.

40. The Hebrew Bible includes of course a mix of unilateral and bilateral discussions of covenant; see, among others, Jon D. Levenson, *Sinai and Zion: An Entry into the Jewish Bible* (San Francisco: Harper & Row, 1987 [1985]). Any creative theological interpretation of this material must offer an ordering of the two different sorts of accounts. I am assuming a unilateral establishment of covenant that sets up a way of life for God's people. The blessings of covenant are conditional on the pursuit of that way of life but not the covenant relationship itself with God, who remains faithful to the covenant, ever calling Israel back to that way of life, which brings with it all the blessings of life.

41. For an account of what Christ is doing on the cross to save us that does not focus in these ways on payment of a penalty or fulfillment of an obligation of obedience, see Kathryn Tanner, "Incarnation, Cross, and Sacrifice: A Feminist-Inspired Reappraisal," *Anglican Theological Review* 86/1 (winter 2004): 35–56.

42. See Sharon H. Ringe, *Jesus, Liberation, and the Biblical Jubilee: Images for Ethics and Christology*, Overtures to Biblical Theology (Philadelphia: Fortress Press, 1985).

43. See Paul F. Camenisch, "Gift and Gratitude in Ethics," *The Journal of Religious Ethics* 9/1 (spring 1981): 26.

44. See ibid., 3–11, 23, for a helpful discussion of responses that might be expected and appropriate without being strictly obligatory.

45. See Lawrence C. Becker, *Reciprocity* (Chicago: University of Chicago Press, 1986), 139.

46. See Camenisch, "Gift and Gratitude," 30.

47. I am disagreeing here with John Milbank. Cf. his "The Ethics of Self-Sacrifice," *First Things* 91 (March 1999): 33–38.

3. Putting a Theological Economy to Work

1. For examples of this sort of position, see the very influential work by Herman E. Daly and John B. Cobb Jr., *For the Common Good: Redirecting the Economy toward Community, the Environment, and a Sustainable Future* (Boston: Beacon, 1989); and Ulrich Duchrow, *Alternatives to Global Capitalism: Drawn from Biblical History, Designed for Political Action* (Utrecht: International, 1998), chapters 4–6, 9. The latter also includes suggestions for global economic reform, but these are given only a very weak religious justification. For a secular version, see Ankie Hoogvelt, *Globalization*

and the Postcolonial World: The New Political Economy of Development, 2nd ed. (Baltimore: John Hopkins University Press, 2001), 263–67.

2. This is the temptation, following the lead of Radical Orthodoxy, of D. Stephen Long, *Divine Economy: Theology and the Market*, Radical Orthodoxy Series (London: Routledge, 2000).

3. This is the classic thesis of Karl Polanyi, *The Great Transformation* (Boston: Beacon, 1957). It is also the hallmark of the French Regulation School (for example, Michel Aglietta and Alain Lipietz). It has become an increasingly commonplace theory among economists. See, for example, the work of the far from radical international political economist Robert Gilpin, *Global Political Economy: Understanding the International Economic Order* (Princeton, N.J.: Princeton University Press, 2001).

4. See Hoogvelt, *Globalization*.

5. See Duchrow, *Alternatives*, 95–97; and International Forum on Globalization Report Drafting Committee, *Alternatives to Economic Globalization* (San Francisco: Berrett-Koehler, 2002), 44.

6. See Joseph E. Stiglitz, *Globalization and Its Discontents* (New York: Norton, 2002), 13, 65; and Samir Amin, *Capitalism in the Age of Globalization: The Management of Contemporary Society* (London: Zed, 1997), 13.

7. See Hoogvelt, *Globalization*, chapters 8–11; and Gøsta Esping-Andersen, *The Three Worlds of Welfare Capitalism* (Princeton, N.J.: Princeton University Press, 1990).

8. See Hoogvelt, *Globalization*, 104–5, 132, 137–38; and Manuel Castells, *The Rise of the Network Society*, 2nd ed., Information Age 1 (Oxford: Blackwell, 2000), 170, 172, 173.

9. See David Harvey, *The Condition of Postmodernity: An Inquiry into the Origins of Cultural Change* (Oxford: Blackwell, 1990), chapter 17.

10. Compare, for example, Daly and Cobb, *For the Common Good*, chapter 11, with Jagdish Bhagwati, *In Defense of Globalization* (New York: Oxford University Press, 2004).

11. United Nations Development Programme, *Human Development Report 1992* (Oxford: Oxford University Press, 1992), 8, 89.

12. See, for example, Stiglitz, *Globalization*; and Amartya Sen, *Development as Freedom* (New York: Knopf, 1999).

13. Stiglitz, *Globalization*, 78–82.

14. See Hoogvelt, *Globalization*, chapter 4.

15. UNDP, *Human Development*, 52.

16. Ibid., 53.

17. Ibid., 38.

18. Ibid., 66.

19. Ibid., 79. See Stiglitz, *Globalization*, chapter 4, on the East Asian financial crisis. Asian nations often had a high rate of savings to fuel investment without requiring foreign funds.

20. See, for example, Stiglitz, *Globalization*, 107–9.

21. See ibid., chapters 4 and 5.

22. UNDP, *Human Development*, 79.

23. Ibid., 75, and Duchrow, *Alternatives*, 96–97.

24. UNDP, *Human Development*, 6.

25. Getting rid of subsidies for domestic food production and eliminating tariffs and quotas on imported foods would hurt big agribusinesses but need not hurt small farmers producing for local sale.

26. International Forum on Globalization Report Drafting Committee, *Alternatives*, 49–51. UNDP, *Human Development*, 62–64. Developed nations are also subject to those WTO stipulations on free trade; they just do not abide by them.

27. Hoogvelt, for example, believes it is. See also Edward W. Soja, *Postmodern Geographies: The Reassertion of Space in Critical Social Theory* (London: Verso, 1989), 105–7.

28. See Amin, *Capitalism*, 33, 97.

29. Linda Gordon, *Pitied but Not Entitled: Single Mothers and the History of Welfare, 1890–1935* (New York: Free Press, 1994), 2.

30. This is one of the major theses, for example, of UNDP, *Human Development*. See also Michel Aglietta, "Capitalism at the Turn of the Century," *New Left Review* 232 (November–December 1998): 43–90.

31. See J. Magnus Ryner, *Capitalist Restructuring, Globalisation and the Third Way*, Routledge Studies in Global Political Economy (London: Routledge, 2002), chapters 2 and 5.

32. Fritz W. Scharpf, "The Viability of Advanced Welfare States in the International Economy," *Journal of European Public Policy* 7/2 (June 2000): 196–97.

33. Ryner, *Capitalist Restructuring*, 29.

34. Scharpf, "Viability," 207.

35. Ibid., 212.

36. Sven Steinmo, "Bucking the Trend? The Welfare State and the Global Economy," *New Political Economy* 8/1 (2003): 43.

37. Ibid.

38. Scharpf, "Viability," 215.

39. Ibid., 219.

40. Even apologists for global capitalism argue this. See Bhagwati, *In Defense*, 98–99, 233–35, 255–56.

41. Ryner, *Capitalist Restructuring*, 49–50.

42. Ibid., 50.

43. See Lizette Alvarez, "Norway Looks for Ways to Keep Its Workers on the Job," *New York Times*, July 25, 2004, A4.

44. David Harvey, "The Geopolitics of Capitalism," in *Social Relations and Spatial Structures*, ed. Derek Gregory and John Urry (New York: St. Martin's, 1985), 130.

45. Summarized well by Ryner, *Capitalist Restructuring*, 42.

46. See Hoogvelt, *Globalization*; and Soja, *Postmodern Geographies*, chapters 4 and 7.

47. See UNDP, *Human Development*, for further comparison of the strengths and weaknesses of developed and developing nations, 4–5, 39–40, 52–53, 64–65.

48. Ibid., 59–60; Hoogvelt, *Globalization*, 41.

49. UNDP, *Human Development*, 62.

50. International Forum of Globalization Report Drafting Committee, *Alternatives*, 49–50.

51. See UNDP, *Human Development*, chapter 5, for greater detail about the following suggestions.

52. Ibid., 65, 69; and Stiglitz, *Globalization*, 60–62.

53. UNDP, *Human Development*, 45–46; and Stiglitz, *Globalization*, 130–31.

54. UNDP, *Human Development*, 62.

55. Ibid., 75–76.

56. See also Bhagwati, *In Defense*, 182–85, for the negative impact on developing nations of pharmaceutical property rights included in TRIPS.

57. Stiglitz, *Globalization*, 108.

58. Ryner, *Capitalist Restructuring*, 39, citing G. Albo, "'Competitive Austerity' and the Impasse of Capitalist Employment Policy," in *The Socialist Register 1994*, ed. Ralph Miliband and Leo Panitch (London: Merlin, 1994), 147.

59. See Hoogvelt, *Globalization*, chapter 5, and David Harvey, *Condition of Postmodernity*, chapters 8 and 9.

60. Hoogvelt, *Globalization*, 224–25.

61. Ibid., 31.

62. Ibid., 39, and Bhagwati, *In Defense*, 56–57, 61, 63, 161–62, 168–69, 179–80.

63. See Kim Moody, *Workers in a Lean World: Unions in the International Economy* (London: Verso, 1997), 130–31.

64. China has done all the things described in this paragraph with great initial success. See Ted C. Fishman, "The Chinese Century," *New York Times Magazine*, July 4, 2004, 24–31.

65. Alain Lipietz, "The Globalization of the General Crisis of Fordism, 1967–84," in *Frontyard/Backyard: The Americas in the Global Crisis*, ed. John Holmes and Colin Leys (Toronto: Between the Lines, 1987), 35.

66. See Robert Brenner, "The Economics of Global Turbulence," *New Left Review* 229 (May–June 1998): 24–29, for this analysis of decline in the rate of profit.

67. D. Leborgne and A. Lipietz, "New Technologies, New Modes of Regulation," *Environment and Planning D: Society and Space* 6/3 (September 1988): 267.

68. Hoogvelt, *Globalization*, 105–6.

69. Lipietz, "Globalization," 52.

70. Hoogvelt, *Globalization*, 118–19, 162.

71. See Joel Kurtzman, *The Death of Money: How the Electronic Economy Has Destabilized the World's Markets and Created Financial Chaos* (New York: Simon & Schuster, 1993), 83–84.

72. Ibid., chapter 11, and Adrian Hamilton, *The Financial Revolution* (New York: Free Press, 1986), 71–4.

73. Hoogvelt, *Globalization*, 87.

74. Ibid.

75. See Stiglitz, *Globalization*, 94–95, on the actual currency crisis in East Asia in the late 1990s.

76. David C. Korten, *When Corporations Rule the World* (West Hartford, Conn.: Kumarian; San Francisco: Berrett-Koehler, 1995), 197.

77. Stiglitz, *Globalization*, 67; and Hoogvelt, *Globalization*, 88–89.

78. Kurtzman, *Death of Money*, 147.

79. See Korten, *When Corporations Rule*, 198.

80. Stiglitz, *Globalization*, chapter 4.

81. Ibid., 100.

82. Ibid., 65.

83. Kurtzman, *Death of Money*, 67–68.

84. Ibid., 229–30, 232.

85. Ibid., 66–67; and Korten, *When Corporations Rule*, 197.

86. Stiglitz, *Globalization*, 66.

87. Ryner, *Capitalist Restructuring*, 45, 53.

88. Kurtzman, *Death of Money*, 238–39; see "Overview" in *The Tobin Tax: Coping with Financial Volatility*, ed. Mahbub ul Haq, Inge Kaul, and Isabelle Grunberg (New York: Oxford University Press, 1996).

89. Kurtzman, *Death of Money*, 238–39.

90. Stiglitz, *Globalization*, 101.

91. Ibid., 92–95.

92. UNDP, *Human Development*, 80.

93. Stiglitz, *Globalization*, 70.

94. UNDP, *Human Development*, 76, 80.

95. Ibid., 79–80.

96. See Daly and Cobb, *For the Common Good*, 52.

97. Ibid., 59.

98. See ibid., 51–58, for a very good introduction to the concept of externalities. For a more technical discussion, see Francis M. Bator, "The Anatomy of Market Failure," *The Quarterly Journal of Economics* 72/3 (August 1958): 351–79.

99. See the enormous literature on collective action, especially William J. Baumol, *Welfare Economics and the Theory of the State*, 2nd ed. (London: London School of Economics, 1965), chapter 12; Mancur Olson Jr., *The Logic of Collective Action: Public Goods and the Theory of Groups*, Harvard Economic Studies 24 (Cambridge, Mass.: Harvard University Press, 1965); and Russell Hardin, *Collective Action* (Baltimore: Johns Hopkins University Press, 1982).

100. Another solution is to encourage voluntary donations from more people through the use of premiums; the promise of benefits that only people contributing

will receive provides the necessary added incentive. Many public radio stations, for example, use this tactic to generate private donations that make up for government funding shortfalls; contributors receive things like mugs or tote bags.

101. See J. G. Head, "Public Goods and Public Policy," *Public Finance* 17/3 (1962): 204.

102. See UNDP, *Human Development*, 84.

103. See Daly and Cobb, *For the Common Good*, chapter 7.

104. UNDP, *Human Development*, 63.

105. Ibid., 2–3.

106. Ibid., 17, 63.

107. Ibid., 18.

108. Ibid., 2, 18.

109. See Head, "Public Goods," 203–5; and also Bator, "Anatomy," 363–65, although he does not class it as a feature of public goods per se.

110. Duncan Snidal, "Public Goods, Property Rights, and Political Organizations," *International Studies Quarterly* 23/4 (December 1979): 537.

111. Ibid., 533.

112. Hoogvelt, *Globalization*, 112.

113. Daley and Cobb, *For the Common Good*, 51; Bator, "Anatomy," 365–71; and Head, "Public Goods," 212–15.

114. Snidal, "Public Goods," 549.

115. Ibid., 532–66. This is the major thesis of the whole article.

116. Mary Douglas, *Risk and Blame: Essays in Cultural Theory* (London: Routledge, 1992), 131; and Hardin, *Collective Action*, 19. See also Head, "Public Goods," 217–18.

117. These similarities are easy to see on a national level following Keynesian principles. In times of recession it would be good for the whole country if businesses increased their investments in technological innovation. Those that did so, however, would risk bankruptcy unless others did likewise. They therefore won't without government encouragement. Head, "Public Goods," 217–18.

118. See Stiglitz, *Globalization*, 12, 224–27.

119. See Moody, *Lean World*, 79, 143–48.

120. Polanyi, *Great Transformation*, 158–63.

INDEX

Printed in the United States
114575LV00002B/55/A